J. SAMUEL WHITE & Co.
SHIPBUILDERS

J. Samuel White & Co.
Shipbuilders

David L. Williams & Richard P. de Kerbrech

The History Press

Above: The Polish destroyer *Blyskawica* (yard No.1801) will forever be associated with Cowes, following her brave defence of the town during an intensive German air raid on the night of 4–5 May 1942. She and her sister *Grom* are probably the finest examples of this type of ship built by the shipyard. The year 2012 has particular significance for her, being the seventy-fifth anniversary of her entry into service in October 1937, as well as the seventieth anniversary of that memorable night when, under the command of Commander Roman Francki, her guns drove off the German bombers bent on destroying the town where she was created. In 1987 the *Blyskawica* was honoured with the Gold Cross of the Military Order Virtuti, the Polish Navy's highest decoration bestowed on a fighting ship. This image shows the *Blyskawica* leaving the River Medina with East Cowes in the background. (Tim Gladdis)

Frontispiece: The launch of the *Sidi Mabrouk* at East Cowes on 24 April 1948. (Keith MacDonald)

First published 2012

The History Press
The Mill, Brimscombe Port
Stroud, Gloucestershire, GL5 2QG
www.thehistorypress.co.uk

British Library Cataloguing in Publication Data.
A catalogue record for this book is available from the British Library.

ISBN 978 0 7524 6612 5

Typesetting and origination by The History Press
Printed in Great Britain

CONTENTS

A portrait of John Samuel White (1838–1915) after whom the combined business was known from around 1860. If not the founder of the famous shipbuilding concern, he was certainly the person responsible for creating the well-remembered modern company. (J. Samuel White Archives)

FOREWORD

The name John Samuel White has been a byword in British and foreign naval construction for many years, hence the saying: 'White's built – Well built!'

During its long history the shipbuilder constructed many ships, including at least fifty destroyers and 285 other naval vessels built throughout two world wars. Among them, worth noting, was the fast minelayer HMS *Abdiel*, designed to appear as a slow 'County'-class cruiser but which could steam off at high speed if the enemy appeared. Likewise, Sir Peter Scott's gunboat *Grey Goose*, built under great secrecy and powered by silent steam turbines, which regularly made the run to Sweden and back to collect valuable ball bearings. She was silent running and could easily outpace the German E-boats. Also, the first all-welded destroyer, HMS *Contest*, produced at White's in 1944, a technique that resulted in faster building times.

Between the wars, a number of frigates and destroyers were built for the Royal and foreign navies. Notably, in 1936–37, the Polish destroyers *Grom* and *Blyskawica* – the latter the saviour of Cowes – were completely designed and built by White's.

Many quality commercial ships were also constructed, including cross-Channel ferries, Trinity House ships, fire floats, paddle steamers, several dear old chain ferries and a large number of lifeboats for the RNLI.

White's, of course, was not without its shortcomings and idiosyncrasies, especially with regard to its practically non-existent health and safety regulations, even beyond the appalling toilet arrangements which have been written about elsewhere. However, we apprentices (for I was one) survived, notwithstanding the traditional ritual of climbing the wooden structure known as the cooling tower where we secured a brass plate at the top just as our peer apprentices expected us to do. We had a thoroughly good training, due in no small part to the foremen, who we always addressed as 'Mr' and never by their Christian names. The foremen, mostly a dour lot but very fair to us, knew their trades backwards and helped to organise the workforce, unlike some of their later counterparts. Incidentally, I started at White's as an office boy in 1938 on the equivalent of 40p per week pay.

After the Second World War, many apprentices from White's went on to greater things in industry and commerce, as well as in the Royal and Merchant Navies. The privileged few who served their time at White's were and are proud to say, 'We served our apprenticeship at John Samuel White's – Shipbuilders.'

It appears that most of the foregoing is about the apprenticeships but none of it would have been possible without the assistance and comradeship of the rest of the skilled workforce, who were always ready to help show you 'the right way to do it'. Many lasting friendships were formed in the yard and it is gratifying after so many years still to exchange greetings when meeting old comrades.

My thanks go to David Williams and Richard de Kerbrech for reviving the history of this world-famed shipbuilder, for whose industry and reputation the townsfolk of Cowes remain as proud as ever.

Ron S. Trowell, C.Eng, M.I.Mech.E
(former Publicity Manager, J. Samuel White & Co. Ltd)

INTRODUCTION

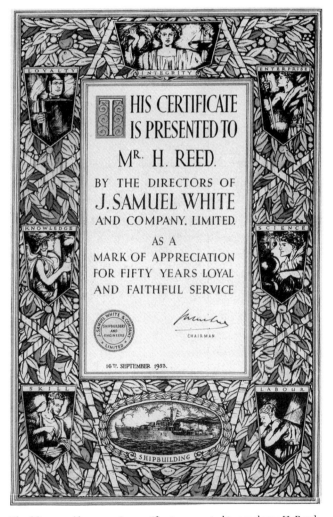

The fifty years' long service certificate presented to employee H. Reed on 16 September 1953. The values promoted by the company are displayed around the frame. (Bernard Taylor)

The history of J. Samuel White & Company, the shipbuilders, the oldest such firm on the Admiralty List, began not on the Isle of Wight where it operated for some 165 or so years, but at Broadstairs in Kent. As far back as the middle of the eighteenth century, White's was already well-established, building Revenue cutters for the Excise service and equally fast craft for smugglers working the Thanet coastline. Sailing yachts also occupied the White concern and John White (1732–1801) was noted for his designs for improved vessels of this type. Before him, an earlier John White (1714–82), his father, in continuing the family's already long tradition of shipbuilding in Kent, had constructed West Indiamen and naval cutters, including HMS *Lapwing* (1764), as well as smacks for local fishermen.

Thomas White (1773–1859), the elder John's grandson, became head of the family concern while still a young man in his twenties, around the time of his father's death. Intent on expanding the shipbuilding business further, he recognised that this would be difficult to achieve in north-east Kent, where the relatively shallow waters inhibited the launching of bigger vessels. So it was, over the early years of the nineteenth century, that he disposed of the shipyard at Broadstairs and progressively moved the business, and his family, to Cowes on the Isle of Wight, where he had acquired suitable premises from other locally established firms.

The records of the company's early years are sparse and obscure, particularly as to which yards on either side of the River Medina were taken over at first, there being great uncertainty in each case as to the precise dates, their exact locations in the absence of maps from the period, and who precisely their former owners had been. In that period it is only possible to provide an indication of the nature, sequence and timescales of events rather than anything more precise or definitive. There have been a number of attempts to unravel the facts of White's inaugural years on the Isle of Wight and the following summary is based upon historical notes and old trade directories. Certainly among the facilities taken over was the former Nye shipyard in East Cowes, which had been building ships for the Royal Navy for more than a century and, in so doing, had already attracted acclaim for its superior building qualities. It is believed that the yard was acquired, after Joseph Nye's death in 1725, by Philomen Ewer, who also had building ways on the River Hamble. Following the death of Ewer in 1783, it was then leased to Robert Fabian, who, according to the *London Gazette*, was bankrupted along with a Samuel Kent on 30 April 1783, although contemporary directories record him, nevertheless, as still running a shipbuilding business in East Cowes more than a year later. He may well have continued to do so until he died in 1788, or the yard may have been the subject of subsequent leases which later expired. It may even have been left idle and abandoned for a period. Either way, at some time around 1800 to 1802 the yard became available for purchase and it was snapped up by Thomas White.

Among the ships built by Nye and his successors was HMS *Poole*, a fifth-rate battleship dating from 1696, and HMS *Jersey*, a fourth-rater built in 1698. When HMS *Vanguard* was launched in 1748, she was the largest ship built on the River Medina up to that date, at 1,419 burthen tons.

The building yard acquired by Thomas White in West Cowes was located in the area now occupied by Shepards Wharf in Medina Road, extending along the shoreline as far as the Point cottages. It was owned by John Gely, who was also declared bankrupt, the impression gained being that shipbuilding in those days was a rather speculative and uncertain business.

The following extract from the *Salisbury & Winchester Journal* of Monday 21 September 1812 details the outcome of his insolvency:

TO SHIP-BUILDERS.
WEST COWES, ISLE OF WIGHT.

TO be SOLD by AUCTION, with immediate possession, by Messrs MEW and PORTER, at the Hotel, West Cowes, on Thursday the 24th day of September, 1812, at four o'clock in the afternoon, (by order of the Assignees of John Gely, a Bankrupt), in such lots and subject to such conditions as will be expressed at the time of sale, - The Reversion in Fee of a very valuable PIECE of GROUND, called the Point, at West Cowes aforesaid, with several very capital STORE-HOUSES thereon erected, and a very convenient Wharf for landing merchandize, a wooden Platform, and Wet Dock, on which the tide flows.

Also a very desirable Freehold brick-built DWELLING-HOUSE, with a good garden and yard adjoining, situated at the Point of West Cowes aforesaid, and for many years past occupied by Mr John Gely, Ship-builder.

If the Close of Land does not sell, it will be offered in lots for building on.

For particulars apply to Mr Worsley, solicitor, Newport, Isle of Wight.

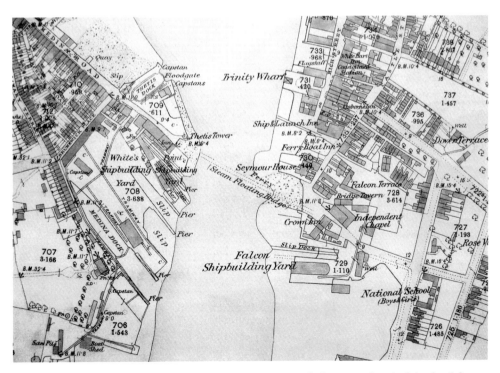

The main shipbuilding business of J. Samuel White & Co. occupied a long stretch on both banks of the River Medina at Cowes. This map, drawn in 1866, shows the two principal areas of the shipyard before it was reorganised to concentrate the building slipways on the East Cowes side, at the Falcon Yard, and the fitting-out quay and engineering works at West Cowes in the Medina Yard. (Authors' collection)

For Thomas White, Gely's financial misfortune had been fortuitous providing the means whereby he was able to secure ship construction facilities on both banks of the River Medina almost from the outset.

While new construction work continued apace in East Cowes, Thomas White set about the enhancement of the West Cowes site, developing an adjacent area of salterns and marshland that characterised the reaches of the West Cowes shoreline in those days. The result was the Thetis Yard, complete with dry dock, which was opened on 1 October 1815. It was the beginning of a process of expansion that would eventually extend to provide spacious and advanced shipbuilding facilities along both shorelines, besides the later addition of an engineering plant, aircraft fabrication works, lifeboat shops, a rope works and other manufacturing, overhaul and repair resources.

The chapters of this book follow the continuing expansion of the White's enterprise through the ensuing years up to and beyond the formation of the J. Samuel White Company, that finally consolidated all the disparate family concerns into a single business which was to continue in existence for over a hundred years to 1974. Presenting the diverse range of products that the company manufactured along with the many design innovations for which

Four new destroyers lie on the West Cowes side in varying stages of completion in this view looking towards the East Cowes slipways dating from 1937. To the left, HMS *Impulsive* is nearest with the *Blyskawica* on her far side; to the right, HMS *Intrepid* is on the inside with the *Grom* on the outside. (Fox Photos; courtesy of Isle of Wight Heritage Service)

This painting shows the 1,419-ton displacement HMS *Vanguard* designed by Sir Jacob Ackworth and built by Ewers in the yard that was taken over by White's. Designated as a third-rate line of battleship with seventy guns, she was the fourth ship in the Royal Navy to bear the name. She was laid down in November 1744 and delivered on 16 April 1748. (J. Samuel White Archives)

it was responsible, some of them patented, this book traces the growth of the various ship construction and engineering operations, along with the commissioning or acquisition of various establishments and premises as the business continued to flourish.

In view of the limitations on space in this publication and given the vast array of the company's products, the illustrations that follow are representative of the output of each period. It was felt necessary in selecting them to focus on as many as possible of the most significant, as well as some of the more unusual engineering activities of J. Samuel White and its subsidiaries.

Above all, this book is intended as a tribute to those thousands of loyal and skilful workers who, over many long years and along with their astute and far-sighted management teams, helped to make J. Samuel White & Co. the illustrious concern it ultimately became and, in so doing, earned for it the enviable worldwide reputation it attained.

Richard P. de Kerbrech & David L. Williams, Isle of Wight, 2012

ACKNOWLEDGEMENTS

We would like to extend our gratitude and thanks to the following persons and organisations for their kindness in contributing information and illustrations, or in providing other help and without whose assistance this publication would certainly not have come to fruition.

Most notably our warmest thanks go to two ladies at the Isle of Wight Heritage Service, Corina Westwood and Caroline Hill, who allowed us unlimited access to the J. Samuel White Archives, extracting pictures and information and who, in so doing, made a major contribution to this work. Our particular gratitude also goes to Ron Trowell, a chartered engineer with White's and the company's former official photographer, both for his help and support, and for supplying the Foreword to this work; many thanks also to Marek Twardowski, curator at the Polish Maritime Museum in Gdynia, for his kind assistance with many of his own photographs, one of which appears on the front cover.

Our thanks also go to Chris Bancroft; John Barrett; Kenneth Beken (Beken of Cowes); Patricia Bochenska MBE; Michael Cassar; Ken Colebrook; Debbie Corner (Royal Navy Submarine Museum); Tim Deacon; Susan Dearing (Fleet Air Arm Museum); the late Alex Duncan; John Edgington; Vicki Gilson (Corporation of Trinity House); Tim Gladdis; Brian Hargreaves and Tony Smith (World Ship Society); Graham Hayes; Kees Helder; David Hutchings; Captain John Landels; Mick Lindsay; Keith MacDonald; Graham Nicholls; Ray Noble; Alan Pearce (Fremantle Harbour Authority); Wayne Pritchett; the late Tom Rayner; David Reed; Nigel Robinson; David Rogers (Massey Shaw Preservation Society); Ted Sandle; Phil Simons; Steve Smith; Richard Smout (Isle of Wight Records Office); Ivy Sulkowska; Ivan Taylor; Adrian Vicary (Maritime Photo Library); Diana Wood; Tony Westmore; the late Kenneth W. Wightman; David Wilkinson, Colin Work and Christine Yendall (Carisbrooke Castle Museum).

Finally we would like to thank two local historians who placed their collections at our disposal: Bernard Taylor and Charlie Taylor.

J. Mortimer Singer's auxiliary schooner *Xarifa* (2) (yard No.1646) off Cowes in August 1927. (Kirk; courtesy of Isle of Wight Heritage Service)

PART ONE

1800-99

The formative years of the White shipbuilding business on the Isle of Wight were characterised by all the major yard developments, which were the fundamental building blocks for the future.

It began with the already mentioned Thetis Yard and dry dock, opened in 1815. In those years, Thomas White's son Joseph was already being acquainted with the workings of the yards and just ten years later, already a partner in the firm, he established a yard of his own in East Cowes for the construction of yachts. Joseph soon gained an enviable reputation for his imaginative and novel designs, and for workmanship that was second to none.

Thomas White's next project was the expansion of the West Cowes premises, involving development of the land to the south of the Point, to create modern shipbuilding facilities with new, longer slipways and, at the extreme end of the site, a second, larger dry dock. This was the new Medina shipyard with its Steam Frigate Dock, a dock which opened on 24 February 1845.

Two of Thomas White's sons by his second marriage, John and Robert, also entered the business. John was a practical shipbuilder and an astute businessman, whereas Robert's strength lay in his enquiring mind. He set about investigating hydrodynamics, ship behaviour and methods of ship construction and for practical experimentation he built a model testing pond in the garden of his father's house, behind the Medina shipyard.

In the entrepreneurial spirit encouraged by their father, John and Robert went on to open a lifeboat-building shop in West Cowes where, in a number of variants, more than 700 of their patented lifeboats were built, the design having been conceived in conjunction with their neighbour Andrew Lamb, the first chairman of what has become Red Funnel Steamers. Carvel-built, on whaler principles and designed primarily to satisfy the demands of the P&O Line, the patented lifeboat had limited self-righting capabilities but, as was stressed by its designers, it was less likely to capsize in the first place. Following the loss of the gunboat *Ariadne* in 1842, the Admiralty insisted that every Royal Navy ship should carry them, accounting for 500 orders, and, although they were designed for shipboard use, many were also supplied to private lifeboat stations for shore deployment.

The patented lifeboat was not the first ground-breaking achievement to the company's credit. Back in 1834, Thomas White had built the earliest steam-powered revenue cutter, the paddle-propelled, 325 burthen tons *Vulcan*.

Following their success with lifeboats, brothers John and Robert next developed a life-saving device for large steamers in collaboration with Captain Hire of the Admiralty Transport Service. The patented Hire & White lifeboat bridge, as it was known, fitted athwartships, allowed boats to be moved to port or starboard for launching in an emergency, according to whichever way a stricken vessel was listing.

Significant among the orders secured in the mid-nineteenth century was a series of large ocean steamers built for the Royal Mail and P&O Lines. These ships featured White's patented system of diagonal planking, which eliminated the need for frame members in the construction of wooden ships, as well as improving their buoyancy and increasing their internal capacity.

By the mid-1800s, it was recorded that the White's shipyards, with their sawmills and engine shops, were collectively employing around 500 craftsmen. It was in this period that White's also won a succession of contracts for ships for Turkish customers, a total of twelve ships for the Ottoman (Turkish) Navy and fourteen ferries for the Bosphorus Steam Navigation Company (Şirketi Hayriye).

In 1860, strongly influenced by John Samuel White, the son of John White, a yard list was started. The young John Samuel, then only twenty-two years of age, was to emerge as the central character directing future company developments, and by 1884 all the disparate parts of White's enterprises had been amalgamated under his name.

The later part of the century was dominated by engineering developments and the commencement of construction of torpedo boats. A large engineering works was opened in 1889 in the West Cowes yard, occupying the site of the Medina dry dock which was purposely filled in. Already, twenty-five years earlier, John Samuel White had begun to develop high-speed steam engines for launches in conjunction with the Birmingham engineer, George E. Belliss. In 1897, Andrew Forster was appointed as Engineering Works Manager. Out of his partnership with John Samuel White, the highly-regarded White-Forster water tube boiler was to be designed and patented.

White's played a prominent part in the development of the naval torpedo boat, not least because of its patented 'Turnabout' concept. The prototype craft with these characteristics, which carried a second rudder permitting the vessel to be stopped dead rapidly or rotated almost about its own length, was built speculatively in 1881. Purchased for HMS *Inflexible*, it led to more orders for various other boats whose designs featured the 'Turnabout' principle and, later, for larger, improved torpedo boats of a type that were derived from those pioneering innovations.

By the turn of the twentieth century, the J. Samuel White Company, across its already diverse operations, was providing work for more than 1,500 local employees.

The Falcon Yard was opened in 1825 under the management of Joseph White. It would eventually become the location of the main shipbuilding slips of the shipbuilders J. Samuel White. This painting shows vessels on the Falcon slips, viewed from the River Medina in the early years of the yard's existence. The berths were ahead of their time in that they provided covered ways, whereby shipwrights and craftsmen could work in all weathers. (Samuel G.T. Williams; courtesy of Bernard Taylor)

The Medina Steam Frigate Dock, started in 1844 and constructed out of wood, was commissioned in a bid to secure the maintenance and overhaul work of East Indiamen bound to and from the Thames. At the time, there were few graving docks in the area, other than for warships in the naval dockyard at Portsmouth. The growth of the port of Southampton from the mid-1800s also offered much potential business for the new dry dock. (Samuel G.T. Williams; courtesy of Bernard Taylor)

LAUNCH OF "THE WATERWITCH," AT COWES.

Designed and built by Joseph White, the ten-gun naval brig *Waterwitch* was completed in 1834. She had originally been ordered as a brig-yacht by the Earl of Belfast and was launched at East Cowes on 18 June 1832, an event recorded in the news journals of the day. Her dimensions of 331 tons, 90ft length and 29ft beam made her the template of future naval brig design. (*Illustrated London News*)

The *Waterwitch* is seen running under full sail in this painting. Lord Belfast persuaded the Admiralty to buy her after she had defeated all naval vessels in friendly races. She had shown she was more seaworthy and comfortable than the twelve-gun so-called 'coffin brigs' in use by the navy at that time and could carry an equally heavy battery and plenty of stores. (Victor Colleypriest; courtesy of J. Samuel White Archives)

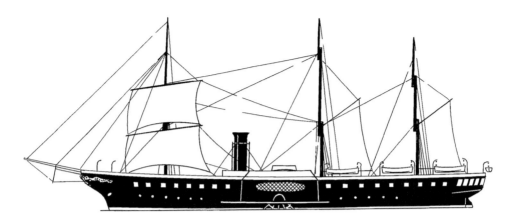

This line profile shows the 1,800-ton wooden paddler *Medina* built by Thomas and John White for the Royal Mail Steam Packet Company. She was launched on 6 July 1841 and engined by Edward Bury of Liverpool with two 200 nhp side lever steam engines. She left on her maiden voyage from Southampton on 27 January 1842, but on the return leg she grounded on a reef off the West Indies on 12 May 1842. (Nigel V. Robinson)

The Thetis Yard in West Cowes, built on reclaimed marshland, had been officially opened on 1 October 1815. As such, this facility established Thomas White's business on both sides of the River Medina. The yard later incorporated a dry dock capable of taking ships up to 800 tons burthen, the only large non-naval dry dock in the area. The picture shows the Thetis Dock in 1845 with an East Indiaman in the new dry dock. (J. Samuel White Archives)

OPENING OF THE NEW STEAM-FRIGATE DOCK, ISLE OF WIGHT.

Work on the Medina Steam Frigate Dock, as it was known, measuring 257ft in length and 62ft in breadth, was started in 1844. P&O Line's *Braganza* was the first ship to enter the Medina dry dock on 24 February 1845, the occasion of the dock's official commissioning. In 1853 the Medina dry dock was extended inland to increase its length to accommodate the new packet steamers being built for P&O and Royal Mail. Later still, from 1889, it was filled in to provide development space for the company's new Engineering Works. (*Illustrated London News*)

The armed steamer *Vasita-i-Tacaret* was one of three early contracts that White's secured from the Ottoman (Turkish) Steam Navy. Ordered and laid down in 1846, she was launched on 1 March 1847 and was of 936 gross tons and a displacement of 1,350 tons. She was of wooden construction, 207ft long and 31ft 4in beam. The *Vasita-i-Ticaret* was a paddle-driven steamship with a single boiler and a single two-cylinder Maudslay engine of 650 ihp. (Authors' collection)

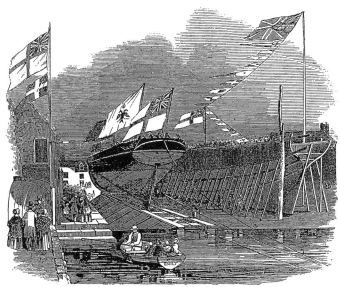

LAUNCH OF THE EMPEROR'S YACHT AT EAST COWES, ISLE OF WIGHT.

Though attributed to Thomas White, the schooner yacht *Queen Victoria*, seen on the slipway at the Gridiron Yard, East Cowes, on the occasion of her launch, was built by Joseph White for Tsar Nicholas I in 1846. A notable feature of the *Queen Victoria* was the saloon which measured 23ft in length, extended across the yacht's full beam and had almost 7ft headroom under the beams. (*Illustrated London News*)

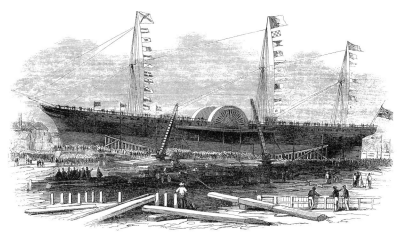

LAUNCH OF THE WEST INDIA MAIL STEAM-SHIP "SOLENT," AT COWES.

Among the innovations introduced by John White in the mid-1800s was a patented diagonal planking system which eliminated the need for frame members in the construction of wooden ships. Patented in 1850 as an improvement on the existing systems of diagonal construction, it required the retention of only the floors and lower futtocks or ribs, with the upper portion of the hull completed by diagonal and longitudinal planking alone. Among its benefits, the new system offered greater internal capacity and improved buoyancy. One of the first vessels built according to White's diagonal planking system was the paddle steamer *Solent*, ordered by the Royal Mail Steam Packet Co. She is seen here on the slipway at T. & J. White prior to being launched on 8 June 1853. (*Illustrated London News*)

At 2,230 tons and 310ft length, the *Solent* was the largest ship so far built by the company. She was fitted out at the West India Dock with twin-cylinder, oscillating, side lever paddle engines manufactured by Miller & Ravenshill. These engines produced 400 hp which gave her a service speed of 12 knots. Her composite construction, with wooden beams constructed on wrought iron frames, was a milestone on the path towards the all-iron built vessels that were then emerging. In her case, the iron frames provided extra rigidity to her long hull. Her maiden voyage commenced on 3 October 1853 from Southampton to the West Indies. (Isle of Wight Heritage Service)

LAUNCH OF THE PENINSULAR AND ORIENTAL COMPANY'S STEAM-SHIP "VECTIS," AT COWES.

On the slipway just prior to her launch on 11 January 1853 is the P&O paddle steam packet *Vectis*. In the background is Royal Mail's *Solent*. The *Vectis*'s 400 hp engines were constructed by Messrs John Penn & Company and she was capable of making 15 knots. The *Vectis* was christened by Thomas White, his appearance at her launch being the last occasion he visited the yard. He died six years later in 1859. (*Illustrated London News*)

P&O Line's *Vectis* and her fleetmate *Tartar*, both attributed to Thomas and Robert White, were built according to the new diagonal planking principles. In this contemporary impression, the *Vectis* can be seen sailing from The Solent, passing the Needles in the background. The *Vectis* served on the Marseilles to Malta and Alexandria route until 1865 when she was sold to the Egyptian Government and renamed *Kalwab*. (P&O Line)

Described as building ships of war in the 1850s, the picture depicts a typical wooden-walled warship of the day in the Medina dry dock, with the pump house to the left and the tower in the garden of Thomas White's house beyond the ship, to the right. (J. Samuel White Archives)

The innovative schooner-rigged opium clipper *Wild Dayrell*, completed in November 1855, was built by Messrs John & Robert White in the Medina Dock as the last of this type for the established firm Messrs Dent & Co. of Hong Kong. She was constructed with extra fastenings and scantlings where required so as to strengthen her for the tempestuous weather of the China Seas. She measured 253 tons by the Old Measurement and was 103ft 4in long overall, with a breadth of 23ft 8in. (*Illustrated London News*)

The shallow draught gunboats *Grinder* and *Jasper* were ordered from John White by the Royal Navy for service in the Sea of Azov, based at Crimea. Delivered in 1855, they measured 232 tons. In this drawing, which shows them under construction on the left, HMS *Tay* may also be seen to the right, in the Medina dry dock. The company declined more gunboat contracts with the Admiralty at that time because all the yard's skilled shipwrights were fully committed. White's was reluctant to take on any work that might result in delayed delivery or inferior quality, a policy that was to remain central to its operating philosophy into the future. (J. Samuel White Archives)

A wooden paddle vessel takes shape on the stocks. The starboard paddle arch and sponson can be clearly seen under construction. The ship is being built in the Medina shipyard with a canvas tarpaulin for weather protection and gaslight so that work could be carried on after dark. (J. Samuel White Archives)

This view of the Medina dock and shipyard dating from 1856 shows a de-masted merchant sailing ship to the left, berthed in the dry dock alongside the prominent pump house. The larger of the two vessels on the slipways could be the 183 gross ton, three-masted schooner *Englishman*, attributed to Hamilton White, which was completed and delivered to Messrs Brufond of Bristol in 1854. (J. Samuel White Archives)

Seen from the opposite direction to the previous picture, the warship HMS *Carnatic* can be seen under repair in the Medina dry dock in this view from 1859. Vague images to the left of the pump house show other new build-ships on the slipways of the Medina shipyard. (J. Samuel White Archives)

The orders for the Brazilian Government included the wooden paddlers *Appa* and *Princeza de Jainville*, to the left of the illustration, designated as 'despatch vessels' and both launched during 1858. They measured 927 tons, with dimensions of 198ft length between perpendiculars, 31ft beam and 7ft 4in draught. Their engines, built by Maudslay, were designed to give a guaranteed speed of 12 knots. To the right, in dry dock, is the 452-ton barque *Charlotte Ann*. (J. Samuel White Archives)

THE IMPERIAL CHINESE DESPATCH-BOAT KEANG-SOO, FLAG SHIP OF CAPTAIN SHERRARD OSBORN, C.B.

One of the largest ships completed by White's in 1862, when the yard was still being run by John White, was the Imperial Chinese paddle despatch vessel, or sloop, *Keang Soo*, measuring 1,018 burthen tons and 242ft in length. Her engines were supplied by Day & Company of Southampton. (*Illustrated London News*)

The Thetis Dock, shown in an impression from 1863, shows the progress of construction in the area since the view on page 21, drawn in 1845. At the centre and to the left are buildings which still exist today: the Bell Inn nearest to the river, now a private residence, and the three-storey buildings which until quite recent times were used as a sail loft by Ratsey & Lapthorn. The turreted Thetis Tower, built in November 1862, was only demolished in July 1975. (J. Samuel White Archives)

The 137 gross ton *Vectis* was originally completed and engined by John White in 1866 and as such was the first paddle steamer built for the newly combined Southampton, Isle of Wight and South of England Royal Mail Steam Packet Co. Ltd, the antecedents of Red Funnel Steamers. Launched on 14 June 1866, she had a 60 ihp engine installed. With a distinctive clipper bow, she had a length of 140ft 8in, but it is thought that her clipper bow was removed around 1888 when she was relegated to cargo work. Simultaneously, her tonnage was reduced to 122 gross tons. (Chris Bancroft)

An early precursor of the wooden steam torpedo boat design, prior to that of the *Swift*, was built by the yard in the 1870s. In some cases steam yachts were built to the later torpedo boat design in order to gain extra speed. A notable example was that of the steam yacht *Scud* (see page 39). (Kirk)

A view of HMS *Euridyce* showing her in the Medina dry dock where she was overhauled. The photograph dates from March 1876. The *Euridyce* was lost in a freak storm in Sandown Bay on 24 March 1878 while returning to Portsmouth from a voyage to the West Indies. (Authors' collection)

The schooner-rigged auxiliary steam yacht *Sunrise* (yard No. 333) was built for Lord Ashburton. As completed, in 1877, she was fitted with Penn compound engines which remained in her through to and beyond 1914, although her boiler was replaced in 1897. She served as a hospital ship during the Boer War. Later, converted to barque rig, she was renamed *Yves de Kerguelen* and again, in 1913, when she became the *Isles de Kerguelen*. (Kirk)

The 125ft 'Turnabout' Torpedo Boat No.34 (yard No.683) was one of five, numbers 34 to 38, delivered to the Royal Navy in 1886–87. The patented 'Turnabout' principle was another of White's innovations in the nineteenth century which, using twin rudders mounted on the centreline of the keel, one aft and one forward of the propellers, gave vessels enhanced manoeuvrability. Torpedo Boat 34 is seen here at the entrance to Cowes harbour. The hole of her torpedo bow discharge gear may be clearly seen in her ram-shaped bow, also the side-dropping gear aft. Although not clearly evident from this view, these torpedo boats in fact had two funnels abreast of each other. (Kirk; courtesy of Isle of Wight Heritage Service)

The steel-hulled steam yacht *Wildfire* (yard No.728) was designed and built by the company in 1887. She was fitted with Bellis engines supplied by the Birmingham concern of George E. Bellis, the yard's main engine supplier at that time prior to the establishment of a local engineering works. (Kirk; courtesy of Isle of Wight Heritage Service)

This luxuriously outfitted 30ft steam pinnace or, more correctly, life cutter (yard No.836) was built by White's for the Russian Royal Family's yacht *Polar Star*. This photograph of her was taken during her sea trials in 1890. (Kirk; courtesy of Isle of Wight Heritage Service)

The *Jere* (yard No.896) and *Paria* (yard No.897) were composite-built paddle steamers for Trinidad, both delivered in 1892. Each measured 120 gross tons, was 110ft long and was fitted with compound steam engines by the builders. (Debenham; courtesy of Isle of Wight Heritage Service)

▲ The torpedo boats of the 94 to 96 series (yard Nos 910–912) delivered in 1894 were a great improvement on contemporary vessels of this type then being built by other shipyards to the same specification. They displaced 130 tons on dimensions of 145ft length by 15ft 7in beam. Fitted with machinery supplied by Maudslay Sons & Field, they achieved a trials speed of 23 knots on 200 hp. (Kirk; courtesy of Isle of Wight Heritage Service)

▼ Torpedo Boat Nos 94–96 were a further development in design from the turnabout boats Nos 34–38, having a straight bow in place of their predecessors' ram bow, and their funnels positioned fore and aft rather than abreast of each other. In addition, the turtle-back forecastle extended aft to the bridge. This view shows Torpedo Boat No.95. (Wayne Pritchett)

The 120-ton steel miner *Sir Charles Pasley* (yard No.915), built for the War Office in 1893, was one of a large number of these craft, constructed in both wood and steel, that were completed by J. Samuel White as precursors to true minelayers. She is seen here moored in the River Medina with the East Cowes yard in the background. Renamed *Redwing*, she became a special service vessel at Portsmouth in 1905. (Isle of Wight Heritage Service)

The steam yacht *Xarifa* (I) (yard No.942), berthed at Cowes in 1894, was a 530-ton, 160ft-long brigantine-rigged vessel of composite construction. She was the first of three yachts that bore the same name that were delivered by White's to Mr F. Mortimer Singer, the owner of the Singer Sewing Machine Company. (Wayne Pritchett)

The first *Xarifa* is seen here under full sail. After a brief spell under the French flag as the *Ophelie*, she reverted to her original name and served as a US Navy auxiliary during the First World War. (Kirk; courtesy of Isle of Wight Heritage Service)

HMS *Conflict*, *Teazer* and *Wizard* (yard Nos 945–947), all 'A'-class ships, were designed with the requirement that they should present as small a target as possible, thus they were of low freeboard. They were 270 tons displacement, 205ft 6in in length and each cost £39,113. They were engined by Maudslay and developed 4,500 ihp which gave them a speed of 27 knots. Their main armament was a single 12-pounder gun on the roof of the conning tower forward and three 6-pounders placed one on each side abaft the turtle back and one aft. Here, HMS *Teazer*, launched on 9 February 1895, is seen alongside the fitting-out quay at West Cowes. (Debenham; courtesy of J. Samuel White Archives)

▲ The *Ardilla* (yard No.976) was one of six gunboats of 43 displacement tons constructed for the Spanish Navy in 1895. The others were the *Alerta, Cometa, Fradera, Golondrina* and *Gaviota*. (Kirk; courtesy of Isle of Wight Heritage Service)

▼ The steel steam yacht *Scud* (yard No.986), built in 1896, was of 45 tons Thames Measurement and 84ft 6in length. She was powered by a White's three-cylinder compound steam engine. Built for Mr A.H. Woods on the lines of a naval torpedo boat, she was designed for high speed. In 1899 she was bought by W.C.S. Connall but by 1902 she had been resold to Thakur Sahib who remained her owner until she was wrecked in 1909. This photograph, showing the *Scud* at high speed, was taken in 1905. (Kirk; courtesy of Isle of Wight Heritage Service)

The auxiliary steam yacht *Hecla* (yard No.990), was designed and built by White's in 1896 for R.A. Johnston of Cowes. She was fitted with White's-built engines and boilers. (Kirk; courtesy of Isle of Wight Heritage Service)

In 1897 the White-Forster water tube boiler was patented. It was named jointly after Andrew Forster, who for many years was White's Engine Works Manager. Essentially, the popular White-Forster boiler was similar in general arrangement to the Yarrow boiler of the day, having two lower water drums connected by generating tubes to an upper steam and water drum, the water level being arranged such that all tubes were flooded. The boiler and its casings were constructed entirely of riveted mild steel; no castings were used. (Authors' collection)

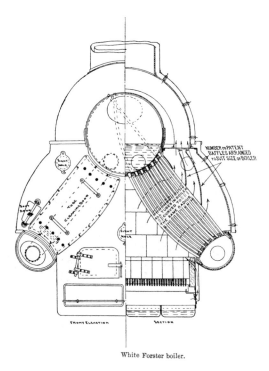

White Forster boiler.

The Boiler Shop in the Engineering Department showing White-Forster boilers in various stages of construction, in this case destined for the Chilean destroyers *Almirante Lynch* and *Almirante Condell* (yard Nos 1362 & 1363). The batches of curved water tubes may be clearly seen connecting the steam drum to the water drums. (Debenham; courtesy of Isle of Wight Heritage Service)

Late in the nineteenth century, White's built two large steam-powered lifeboats for the RNLI, the *James Stevens No. 3* and *No. 4* (yard Nos 1054 and 1055), one of which is seen here. These boats had their propeller placed in a tunnel in the aft part of the hull to reduce racing when pitching in heavy, head-on seas. *No. 3* was based at Grimsby and *No. 4* at Padstow. (Maltby & Warner; courtesy of Isle of Wight Heritage Service)

This rather unique craft is the 'Duck Punt', a steam-driven vessel especially built for Hamilton White around 1899. Notwithstanding the sporting-sounding name of the craft, the weapon it mounted was known as a 'Duck Gun', a large calibre gun of great accuracy, akin to an elephant gun. (J. Samuel White Archives)

One of four 56ft vedettes or steam pinnaces (yard Nos 1071 to 1074) completed in 1900 for Armstrong, Whitworth & Co., on behalf of the Japanese Navy. Here one of them is seen on trials in The Solent prior to delivery. Craft of this type, referred to variously as vedettes, pinnaces or cutters, represented a significant proportion of the yard's output for over twenty years. (Debenham; courtesy of Isle of Wight Heritage Service)

PART TWO

1900-18

The period from the start of the twentieth century to the end of the Great War, as it was then known, witnessed the transition of the White's business into a leading manufacturing concern. Over the twenty years from 1898 when J. Samuel White's had been made a private limited liability company, registered on 11 February 1898, the shipyard's output migrated from predominantly small craft to what were generally large, ocean-going vessels. Simultaneously, the company established itself beyond question as a naval constructor of the highest standing, undertaking the production of warships of the latest type to the most modern designs.

Following the appointment of Edwin Carnt, an engineer of great reputation, as a company director that same year, the engineering works too had gone from strength to strength. The already well-regarded White-Forster water tube boilers were produced in increasing numbers, compound and triple-expansion steam reciprocating engines were being made for other yards, while construction of steam turbines began in a dedicated shop under licence to the Parsons Engine Company. White's was something of a pioneer in the manufacture of internal combustion engines, both petrol and diesel fuelled, supplying its first units for marine application within years of Burmeister & Wain completing the first sea-going motor ship *Selandia* in 1912. By the end of the First World War, the company was offering a complete range of engine products for purchase.

In keeping with the spirit of the age and the desire of the company's directors to be at the forefront of engineering developments, the bold step was taken to open an Aviation Department on 1 January 1913, at a time when aeroplane design was still in its infancy. Another leading light was engaged by the company to head the new venture, the designer Howard Theophilus Wright, who had effectively served his apprenticeship under the guidance of the great early aviator Hiram Maxim. Originally based in the Gridiron Yard at East Cowes, the department was moved to the southern end of the West Cowes facility as serious aircraft production got underway. Later, from 1917, it was transferred to new purpose-built workshops at Somerton when fabrication of landplanes commenced, augmenting the existing production line of seaplanes.

The shipyard facilities also benefitted from steady investment throughout the period, highlighted by the erection in West Cowes of the 80-ton hammerhead crane purchased from Babcock & Wilcox of Renfrew, Scotland. It was part of a major programme of shipyard enhancements to enable the company to take full advantage of the burgeoning worldwide demand for destroyers. The work involved the reclamation of additional land along the river frontage at West Cowes and the filling in of the remaining dry docks, increasing the length of the fitting-out quay to around 600ft. Between 1905 and 1911, twenty-five destroyers were completed. Many more orders for these warships were to follow.

By the end of the First World War, the yard had a nominal capacity of eight building berths, the largest able to take a 350ft-long hull. The old 350ft patent slip was modified to increase its lifting power to 1,000 tons and it was also made convertible to act as a dock that could accommodate vessels up to 240ft length. Two additional patent slips were commissioned.

Meanwhile, berths 2 and 4 had been reconstructed in concrete. There were new steel building sheds with overhead electric travelling cranes, in which new machinery of all types was installed. A new timber store was completed in West Cowes, near the end of Pelham Road, and a new electrical jib crane was added at the end of the North Pier, East Cowes.

By that date, annual output of the shipyard was well in excess of 20,000 tons, more than three times its 1914 level, while that of the engine works, both for other shipbuilders as well as to the company's own account, had grown to the equivalent of 180,000 ihp.

Most impressive was the company's contribution to the national war effort between September 1914 and November 1918, as detailed in the *Isle of Wight County Press* in April 1919. It included those ships that were commenced before the end of hostilities and those completed after the Armistice:

Twenty-six destroyers, beginning with four of the six large destroyers that had been on order for Chile but which were completed as flotilla leaders for the Royal Navy: *Faulknor*, *Broke*, *Botha*, *Tipperary*, *Lightfoot*, *Magic*, *Moresby*, *Medina*, *Medway*, *Sable*, *Setter*, *Trenchant*, *Tristram*, *Vampire*, *Vectis*, *Vortigern*, *Winchelsea*, *Winchester*, *Tribune*, *Trinidad*, *Trojan*, *Truant*, *Trusty*, *Wyvern*, *Wolverine* and *Worcester*.

Two submarines: *E32* and *F2*.

Eleven patrol boats and Q-ships: *P11*, *P12*, *P40*, *P52*, *P59*, *P67*, *P68*, *PC71*, *PC72*, *PC73* and *PC74*.

More than sixty steam pinnaces, barges, motor boats and cutters for the Admiralty and War Office.

A total of 211 aircraft – sixty-seven to White's designs, thirty-four to Admiralty designs and 110 under contract to Shorts Aircraft Company, Rochester.

Apart from the machinery supplied for the ships and other craft built in the yard, the engineering works fabricated main engines for other Royal Navy and Imperial Japanese Navy ships, engines for kite balloon winches, boilers for British and Colonial ships, condensers for patrol vessels and around 1,000 hand-operated oil fuel pumps.

Repair and overhaul work was another major activity and among the ships handled were the Yarrow-built destroyer HMS *Lurcher*, the Fairfield-built destroyer *Melpomene* and the patrol vessel *P24*.

Considering the limited land space available to the shipyard premises on either bank of the River Medina, the quantity and variety of White's wartime output was nothing short of phenomenal.

The single low point for the company during those momentous years was the death in May 1915, aged seventy-four, of John Samuel White, its inspirational leader for almost fifty years. The shipyard was to retain his illustrious name even though all family links with the business were severed soon afterwards. On the plus side, thanks to John Samuel's inspired leadership, the number of craftsmen employed in the business, which had stood at around 2,000 in 1914, had practically doubled by the time the Armistice was declared.

Another quality product of White's was the *Zaida* (yard No.1098), a twin-screw steel steam yacht, built for Mr. A. Shuttleworth of Cowes in 1900. She was schooner-rigged, of 255 gross tons and 145ft overall length, and her pronounced clipper bow was decorated in gold filigree. Designed with excellent sea-keeping qualities, she made a number of long, deep-sea cruises. In 1908 she was sold to the Earl of Rosebery, Commodore of the Royal Fowey Yacht Club, and remained in his ownership until 1915. She was taken up for service on 26 May 1916 by the Royal Navy as an auxiliary patrol vessel and then, armed with two 6-pounder guns, deployed to the eastern Mediterranean. On 17 August 1916 she was attacked and sunk by gunfire from the German submarine *U-35* near Alexandria. (Kirk; courtesy of Isle of Wight Heritage Service)

The triple expansion steam engines, designed and built by White's for the steam yacht *Zaida* (yard No.1098), photographed prior to installation. Triple expansion engines became standard in most steam yachts by the 1890s. With the development of high-pressure boilers it was possible for the compound engine to progress to three cylinders of high, medium (or intermediate) and low pressures. The working action of this type of engine developed less vibration, gave an increase in speed and greater economy of steam usage. The *Zaida*'s cylinder bores were 11, 17 and 26 in with a combined stroke of 20in. (Debenham; courtesy of Isle of Wight Heritage Service)

The 870-ton yacht *Ivy*, built by Earle's of Hull, was one of a number of vessels of this type that were either refurbished or stretched by White's during the years prior to the First World War. (Kirk)

The *Karonga* (yard No.1104), together with her sister *Kampala* (yard No.1103), were a pair of stern-wheeler steamers ordered and completed for the Crown Agents in 1900. They were 75ft long and of shallow draught for use in the rivers of southern Nigeria. Apart from passengers and cargo they were also required to transport livestock. (Debenham; courtesy of Isle of Wight Heritage Service)

Another stern-wheel river steamer built for the Crown Agents in northern Nigeria, the 177-ton *Sarota* (yard No.1122) was delivered in 1902. She and the *Valiant* (see page 48) each had two stern wheels separated by a rudder, although it is unlikely that they operated independently. (Wayne Pritchett)

The 50ft wooden miner *Rodney* (yard No.1148), photographed in the River Medina looking towards West Cowes, was delivered to the Secretary of State for War in 1902. Her swan-neck hoist for mine handling, characteristic of these vessels, is conspicuous. (J. Samuel White Archives)

An atmospheric photograph of the stern-wheeler *Valiant* (yard No.1149), venting steam from her paddle engine and lifting her safety valves. She was completed for the Crown Agents in 1902 and was a further development of her sister ferry, the *Sarota* (yard No.1122). (Debenham; courtesy of Isle of Wight Heritage Service)

The *Lady Forrest* (yard No.1154) was intended for service not only as a lifeboat but also as a pilot and salvage vessel. The photograph shows her early in her career, as completed, when first delivered to the Western Australian Government. She continued in service after considerable modification well into the 1960s. (Alan Pearce, Fremantle Port Authority)

The four torpedo boats, numbers 114–117 (yard Nos 1155–1158), were a class that measured 205 displacement tons. Their coal-fired steam reciprocating engines developed 2,900 ihp driving a single screw, giving them a speed of 25 knots. They each carried three 3-pounder guns and three 14in torpedo tubes. (Debenham)

Torpedo Boat No.116 (yard No.1157) was launched on 21 December 1903. Along with her sisters she was an improvement on the earlier batches of torpedo boats, with a displacement tonnage of 205 tons and a length of 165ft. Their reciprocating machinery had been standardised in accordance with Admiralty specifications such that spares and major units were interchangeable. (Debenham; courtesy of Isle of Wight Heritage Service)

The series of 56ft vedette boats or pinnaces of the 562–569 series (yard Nos 1169–1176), one of which is shown here, were completed for the Admiralty in 1904. (Isle of Wight Heritage Service)

Admiralty Steam Launch No.63 (yard No.1177) was a 60ft, steam-driven launch delivered to the Royal Navy in 1903. She was specifically ordered for the use of the cadets at Osborne Naval College to give them first-hand knowledge of handling small boats at sea. (Kirk)

Though built to an Admiralty specification, builders were allowed considerable latitude in their interpretation of the requirements for the 'River'-class destroyers. Hence, in the *Ness* and *Nith* (yard Nos 1199 and 1212), the latter shown here, the pair completed by White's in August and October 1905, the forward 6-pounder guns were placed on the forecastle deck alongside the bridge rather than on the main deck on sponsons. (Debenham; courtesy of J. Samuel White Archives)

During 1906, White's launched a new series of five coastal destroyers. They were HMS *Cricket*, *Dragonfly*, *Firefly*, *Sandfly* and *Spider* (yard Nos 1223- 1227). All were of 225 tons displacement and 175ft long, but larger and more seaworthy than contemporary torpedo boats. If built to the same Admiralty specification as the five 'Gadfly'-class from Thornycroft at Southampton, it is believed that these may well have been the first turbine driven warships built by White's and the first to be oil-fired. As most of the additional space was occupied by the Parsons turbines, the two water-tube boilers and bunker with its capacity for 20 tons of furnace fuel oil, there was little in the way of space or comfort for the thirty-five crew who nicknamed them 'oily wads'. The turbines developed 3,750 shp on three shafts which gave them a speed of 26 knots. They were armed with two 12-pounders and three 18in torpedo tubes. Although classed as coastal destroyers they were later re-rated as torpedo boats and given changed pennant numbers. Although they gave shipyard staff early experience with turbines and oil fuel, they generated lots of smoke because the stokers were inexperienced with primitive oil-burning equipment. (J. Samuel White Archives)

The first ocean-going destroyer of the 'Tribal' or 'F'-class built by the company was the *Mohawk* (yard No.1228) fitted with White's-built Parsons turbines. She and her later sisters were of a White's design influenced by the ideas of Admiral Sir John Fisher. They had to be capable of: (a) steaming at 33 knots for eight hours in a moderate sea; (b) being oil-fuelled; (c) carrying two 12-pounder guns; and (d) carrying seven days' provisions. *Mohawk*'s trials speed of 34.3 knots, achieved off Maplin Sands, exceeded the contract requirement by almost 1.5 knots. When she returned to The Solent she was sporting a traditional fighting cock pennant at her masthead to signify a speed record. (Authors' collection)

This picture shows Coastal Destroyer No.15 (yard No.1255) one of a further group of four coastal destroyers (yard Nos 1253–1256) which were launched for the Royal Navy in the latter half of 1907. They were slightly improved on the five previous coastal destroyers in that their displacement had been increased to 260 tons and their length to 185ft. In the latter four power output had also risen to 4,000 shp and there was an increased oil bunker capacity of 24 tons. (Maritime Photo Library)

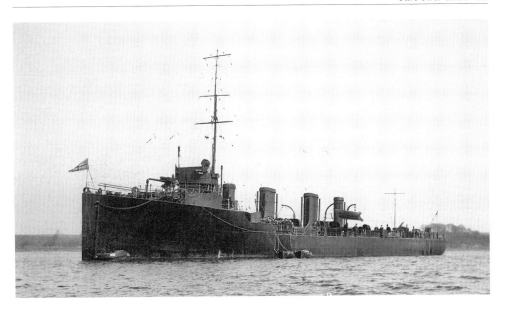

A further development of the *Mohawk* and *Saracen*, the second of the class, the *Crusader* (yard No.1275) was the final 'Tribal'-class destroyer to be built by White's, completed in October 1909. In spite of the cruising turbines, the *Mohawk* and her near sisters were voracious oil consumers with very low endurance. This class mounted two 4in guns and their forward funnel was later heightened so that fumes cleared the bridge. The 'Tribal'-class destroyers cost an average of £137,000 each. (Authors' collection)

HMS *Ruby* (yard No.1317) seen underway. As the last of three 'H' or 'Acorn'-class destroyers, she was launched on 14 November 1910. Her sisters were the *Redpole* (yard No.1315) and *Rifleman* (yard No.1316). At 240ft overall length they were some 35ft shorter than 'G'-class ships, launched earlier in the same year. Although intended to have a speed of 27 knots, during trials *Ruby* achieved 29.3 knots. (Silk; courtesy of J. Samuel White Archives)

The destroyers *Ferret*, shown here, and *Forester* (yard Nos 1322 and 1323) of the 'Acheron'-class, both completed in 1911, were the last destroyers built for the Royal Navy until construction to the order of the Admiralty resumed during the First World War. Having expressed its reservations about the 'regressive' design of these ships, a standard design specified by the Director of Naval Construction, the yard was in effect 'punished' by being excluded from subsequent tenders. The *Ferret* was launched on 12 April 1911 and the *Forrester* on 1 June. They were 246ft long and had twin shafts. Their engines developed 15,000 shp giving a speed of 28 knots. (J. Samuel White Archives)

During 1911 White's delivered three 30ft steam launches (yard Nos 1330–1332) to the Rio de Janeiro Customs in Brazil. Note the framework above the passengers, to support a canvas awning or tarpaulin in place during hot weather. (Kirk; courtesy of Isle of Wight Heritage Service)

The *Diez de Octubre* (yard No.1336), shown here, was one of a pair of gunboats ordered by the Cuban
Navy, the other being the *Viente Cuatro de Febrero* (yard No.1337). Delivered in 1911, these 218-ton
displacement craft were intended to double up as tugs. Their compound steam engines and boilers were
constructed and supplied by the company. (Isle of Wight Heritage Service)

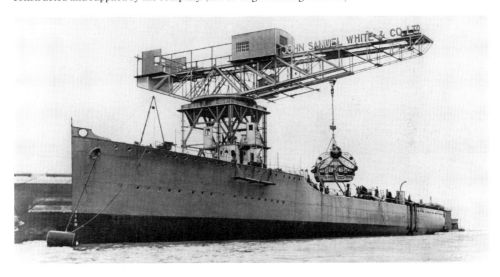

The destroyer *Almirante Lynch* (yard No.1362), seen fitting out alongside the shipyard's West Cowes quay,
is having her boilers lowered into place by the hammerhead crane. The order for six super-destroyers
for the Chilean Navy more than compensated for lost Royal Navy work, while it was also an emphatic
endorsement of the company's reputation with vessels of this kind. As it turned out, four of the six ships
were to enter service with the Royal Navy, taken over prior to completion on the outbreak of the First
World War. (Isle of Wight Heritage Service)

The 80-ton, twin-screw steel motor yacht *I Wonder* (yard No.1371) was designed, built and engined by the firm for Mr John Lee White, John Samuel White's oldest son. She is seen here on trials in 1912. Her engines were twin White 2-stroke, six-cylinder single-acting diesels developing 150 bhp each, giving a maximum speed of 13 knots. (Debenham; courtesy of Isle of Wight Heritage Service)

The J. Samuel White Aviation Department, the inspiration of engineer and director Edwin C. Carnt, was opened in January 1913. The first aircraft to be designed and built by the new department was the Hydro-Aeroplane, or Wight No.1 Seaplane, which was launched into the River Medina from the Gridiron Yard, East Cowes, just four months later, on 5 May 1913. (Authors' collection)

The Gridiron Yard was situated just north of and adjacent to the Cowes floating bridge on the East Cowes side of the River Medina. Formerly operated as a boat-building facility by Joseph White it became the company's first aircraft production site. Once the company's aircraft production began to gain momentum, the Gridiron Yard, which remains in existence to this day as a listed building, was disposed of and manufacturing was transferred across the River Medina to Cowes. (David L. Williams)

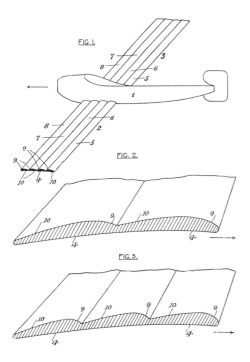

Known as the double camber wing, White's patented wing, conceived by the new Aviation Department's Chief Designer and General Manager, Howard Theophilus Wright, exhibited a multi-curvature, corrugated top surface from the leading to the trailing edge. Intended to increase lift, the wing had only limited application and contributed little benefit to aircraft performance. (Authors' collection)

150-H.P. TWO-CYCLE MARINE DIESEL ENGINE

J. SAMUEL WHITE AND CO., LIMITED, COWES, ISLE OF WIGHT, ENGINEERS

(For description see page 59)

This advert dating from 1913 shows the J. Samuel White 150 hp, six-cylinder, 2-stroke cycle marine diesel engine which had a bore of 7in and a stroke of 16in. This compact and maintenance-accessible engine was built at the company's engine works for installation into craft built in the yards and supplied to other shipbuilders for vessels like tugs, ferries and fishing boats of the time. An engine of this type and horse power was installed and trialled in John Lee White's twin screw motor yacht *I Wonder* (yard No.1371). It is perhaps remarkable that a relatively small firm like White's should 'seize the nettle' of this fledgling means of prime mover, considering that the use of internal combustion engines had not been widely employed on ocean-going ships until the *Selandia* of the Danish East Asiatic Company entered service in 1912. (Authors' collection)

Built for the London County Council in 1913 was the motor-engined fire-float *Delta II* (yard No.1383). Her engines were Kromhout diesels. Measuring 100ft in length by 21ft beam, she had a draught of only 2ft. Her triple screws, fitted in tunnels, gave her a speed of 10 knots. (Real Photos)

In 1912 Chile had ordered six super destroyers or flotilla leaders to White's designs. The first four, launched between February 1914 and March 1915, were the *Almirante Simpson, Almirante Goni, Almirante Williams Robelledo* and *Almirante Riveros* (yard Nos 1366–1389). At 320ft in length they were, with the exception of HMS *Swift*, the world's largest destroyers. Two had been delivered in 1913. Of the remaining four, two were completed in August and November 1914, just as the First World War had broken out, and two the following year. All four were requisitioned by the Admiralty to become HMS *Botha, Broke, Faulknor* and *Tipperary*. The photo shows HMS *Broke* (ex-*Almirante Goni*) undergoing trials. (William Robertson; courtesy of Isle of Wight Heritage Service)

One of the former Chilean super-destroyers, the flotilla leader HMS *Faulknor*, ex-*Almirante Simpson* (yard No.1386), was delivered just twenty days after the outbreak of the First World War. She was distinguished for leading the attack on the German 2nd Battle Squadron at the Battle of Jutland. (Authors' collection)

Another of the 'Broke'-class ships, HMS *Botha* is seen at high speed on builder's trials. (Crown Copyright)

This picture shows the side view of a six-cylinder White-Diesel Engine. This engine, thought to have been built in 1917, has a smoother more compact finish indicating the improvements and accessibility incorporated in the design of diesels since 1913. Confidence and orders in this type of engine supplied by the company must have been high, especially when one considers the foundry casting production included the firm's name on the bedplate. Although the engine appears to be painted white, a cream/ light buff colour was favoured by engine builders of the day. (Isle of Wight Heritage Service)

A development of the one-off No.2 Navyplane, serial number 884, itself a derivative of the original Wight Seaplane No.1, was the Wight Enlarged Navyplane which appeared in April 1914. Seven examples of the type were constructed. Ironically, with war with Germany threatening, four were sold to the German Navy! In the event their delivery was blocked by the company. (Authors' collection)

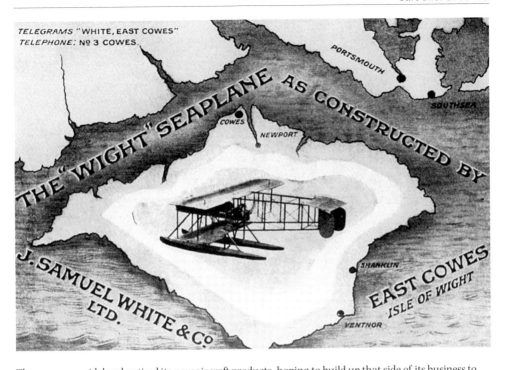

The company widely advertised its new aircraft products, hoping to build up that side of its business to a volume comparable with the shipyard. This advertisement for the Wight Seaplane dates from around 1913. (Authors' collection)

HMS *Laurel* (yard No.1390), an 'L' or 'Laforey'-class destroyer, was launched on 6 May 1913 as the *Redgauntlet*. She is seen here during acceptance trials under her original name and is flying the builder's house flag from her stern. Her sister was HMS *Liberty* (yard No.1391) which had started life as the *Rosalind*. Both vessels were of 995 tons displacement, 320ft in length, twin screw and with an engine power of 22,500 shp. (Cribb; courtesy of J. Samuel White Archives)

One of the most successful home-grown aircraft designs developed by the company was the Type 840 seaplane, a tractor biplane with a long slab-sided fuselage and stepped floats. Its upper wing extended beyond the lower one to improve its aerodynamic characteristics and, powered by a single 225hp air-cooled Sunbeam engine, it had a speed of 75mph. It suited several applications, principally torpedo bomber and reconnaissance seaplane. The Admiralty initially ordered thirty machines and offered White's a follow-on order for an additional fifty-two aircraft. White's was unable to accept the supplementary contract, though, because it had insufficient workshop capacity. (Crown Copyright)

The demand for White's-built aircraft, of which some 211 in total were constructed, caused the company to seek alternative premises to meet the wartime demand. To this end they acquired 60 acres of arable land on the outskirts of Cowes, for the development of an aerodrome. To the east of this they acquired an additional 20 acres, on the east side of the main Newport Road where the hangar and workshops of Somerton Works were built in April 1917. Following the war, all aircraft production ceased in April 1919 and the Aircraft Department was officially closed down on 28 July that year. The Somerton Works, however, remained in White's ownership until 1969. This view is taken from the east side, showing the main building and the sports pavilion. (David L. Williams)

One of the two submarines built by White's during the First World War was the *E32*, seen here. 'E'-class submarines were of 725/810 tons displacement and 181ft 3in in length. They had diesel electric propulsion rated at 1,600 bhp and 840 shp giving them a speed of 16 knots on the surface and 10 knots submerged. Their armament was one 12-pounder and five 18in torpedo tubes. (Cribb; courtesy of Isle of Wight Heritage Service)

White's built only two submarines during the First World War and this view shows one of them under construction in a rather makeshift covered slipway at East Cowes, which was demolished in the early 1920s. A purpose-built structure built later was known as the 'Submarine Shed' even though no submarines were ever built there. The photograph shows the frame stations erected ready for the fitting of the pressure hull. (Cribb; courtesy of Isle of Wight Heritage Service)

The AD Type 1000, or AD Type 1 seaplane, code-named the 'King Cormorant', was the largest aircraft built by J. Samuel White with a wingspan of over 100ft. Designed by Harris Booth at the Admiralty, it was a twin fuselage biplane with three engines, one in each fuselage driving a tractor propeller and a third in a centrally located nacelle driving a pusher propeller. Alongside the AD Type 1000, providing an idea of the scale of the bigger machine, is the 30ft wingspan Baby Trainer Seaplane. Note the additional floats supporting the tail end of each fuselage of the AD Type 1000. (Crown Copyright)

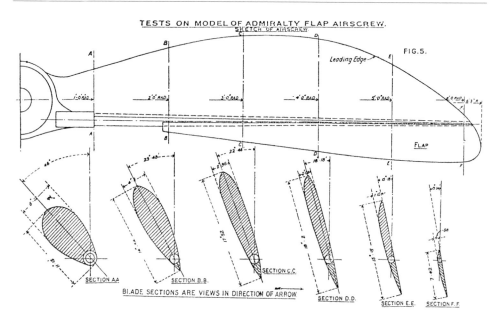

A feature of the AD Type 1000 was its 12ft White's-designed patented flap airscrews or aileron propellers as they were described. They were complicated structures which were designed to permit pitch adjustment to provide enhanced lift at take-off. (Authors' collection)

The very sleek-looking patrol warship *P59* (yard No.1485), built by White's with four other craft of the type between 1916 and 1917, was essentially a submarine destroyer. These vessels were given a very distinctive shape, their low profile, angled funnel and downward sloping aft end intended to create the illusion of a submarine, such that enemy U-boats could be lured to within the range of the patrol vessels' superior fire power. (Crown Copyright)

Originally named *Redmill* and designated as an emergency destroyer, the appropriately named HMS *Medina* (yard No.1467) was launched on 8 March 1916. She was the penultimate destroyer of four 'M'-class ships that White's built. She measured 1,108 tons displacement and 265ft in length. Others of the class were HMS *Magic*, *Moresby* and *Medway* (yard Nos 1455, 1456 and 1468). All four destroyers were completed between January and August 1916, an indication of both the quantity and speed of output of the yard in support of the nation's war effort. (Cribb; courtesy of J. Samuel White Archives)

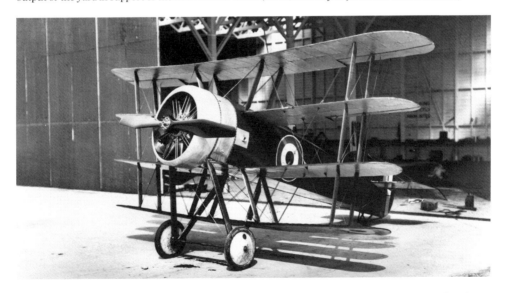

One of only two true landplane aircraft built by White's, that is with wheeled undercarriage rather than floats, this is the unusual, four-winged Quadruplane, seen outside the new aircraft factory at Somerton airfield. Only two Quadruplanes were built as the design was ineffective, any improvements to their aerodynamic qualities being offset by the increase in all-up weight. A replica of Quadruplane N546 can be seen in the Solent Sky Museum, Southampton. (Crown Copyright)

▲ Another highly successful aircraft variant designed by Howard T. Wright was the Wight Landplane Bomber powered by a single 275hp Rolls-Royce engine. Despite the fact that the prototype crashed on 7 September 1916, killing both pilots, the Admiralty was impressed by the aircraft and ordered twenty production machines. Although only five were actually completed (see page 78), the order had been the catalyst for the company's decision to open a new, dedicated aircraft works at Somerton. (Fleet Air Arm Museum)

▼ HMS *Sable* and *Setter* (yard Nos 1477 and 1478) were a pair of 'R'-class destroyers delivered on 30 November 1917 and 12 February 1918 respectively. They were each 265ft long with a displacement of 1,036 tons. This class, which mounted their guns forward, amidships and aft, would be the last in which the armament could all bear on the broadside although it left wide arcs over the bow and stern covered only by a single gun. They embodied improvements in hull and machinery and were fitted with geared turbines which proved a very successful innovation. During steam trials on 13 April 1918, the *Sable* achieved a maximum speed of 35.2 knots. Later, she provided escort assistance to the surrendered German Battle Fleet. Upon completion she was given pennant number G91 but in this photo it has been changed to G44. (Maritime Photo Library)

▼ The Wight Baby Trainer Seaplane, developed for training aircrews for the rapidly expanding Royal Naval Air Service was not taken up by the Admiralty to the extent that the company had hoped. Only three were constructed, one of which is seen here in the River Medina with the East Cowes shipyard in the background. (Crown Copyright)

▲ An advertisement for White's, dating from 1917, shows the Wight Converted Seaplane. Note how these early seaplanes had floats at the ends of their lower main wing. (Authors' collection)

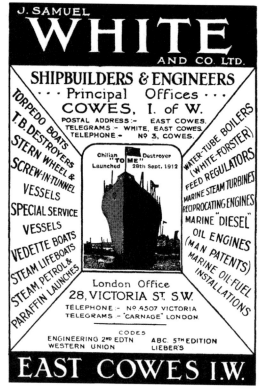

J. SAMUEL
WHITE
AND CO. LTD.

SHIPBUILDERS & ENGINEERS

··· Principal   Offices ···

COWES, I. of W.

POSTAL ADDRESS :–   EAST COWES.
TELEGRAMS :– WHITE, EAST COWES.
TELEPHONE –   N⁰ 3, COWES.

TORPEDO BOATS
T.B. DESTROYERS
STERN WHEEL &
SCREW-IN-TUNNEL
VESSELS
SPECIAL SERVICE
VESSELS
VEDETTE BOATS
STEAM LIFEBOATS
STEAM, PETROL &
PARAFFIN LAUNCHES

Chilian "TOME" Destroyer
Launched   28th Sept. 1912

WATER-TUBE BOILERS
(WHITE-FORSTER)
FEED REGULATORS
MARINE STEAM TURBINES
RECIPROCATING ENGINES
MARINE "DIESEL"
OIL ENGINES
(MAN PATENTS)
MARINE OIL-FUEL
INSTALLATIONS

London Office
28, VICTORIA ST. S.W.
TELEPHONE :– N⁰.4507 VICTORIA
TELEGRAMS – 'CARNAGE' LONDON.

CODES
ENGINEERING 2ᴺᴰ EDTN   ABC. 5ᵀᴴ EDITION
WESTERN UNION   LIEBER'S

EAST COWES I.W.

▲ As it turned out, the aircraft that was to be constructed most prolifically by White's was not one of its own designs. A total of 110 of Shorts 184 seaplanes were built in a new construction shop alongside the West Cowes shipyard that was later to become one of the two boat shops in that area. The Shorts 184 had a wingspan of 63ft 6in and a speed of around 90mph. Like the AD Type 1000, it had skid-type floats. The example shown here is on the slipway outside the West Cowes production shop. (Crown Copyright)

◀ This shipyard advertisement from around the First World War period provides a good indication of the wide range of products, engineering and shipbuilding activities undertaken by J. Samuel White & Co. at this time. Total employees were then approaching 5,000 but this number would reduce as war production wound down. (Isle of Wight Heritage Service)

J. SAMUEL WHITE & C.º L.ᵀᴰ..

MAKERS OF
The "WHITE-BRONS" Oil Engine.

Suitable for :

**WIRELESS SETS,
EMERGENCY
LIGHTING SETS,
DYNAMOS,
COMPRESSORS,
PUMPS and
OTHER
AUXILIARIES.**

**NO HOT BULBS,
VAPOURISERS, or
IGNITION GEAR
REQUIRED WITH
THIS ENGINE.**

*Descriptive
Pamphlet on
application.*

HEAD OFFICE
EAST COWES, I.W.
Telephone : No. 3 Cowes.
Telegrams : '' White, East Cowes.''

LONDON OFFICE
28 VICTORIA
STREET
Telephone : No. 4507 Victoria.
Telegrams:'' Carnage.London.''

This 1917 advert for the White-Brons oil engine boasts its versatility: useful as a prime-mover for small generators, emergency generators, compressors and pumps, and its simplicity and user friendly attributes: 'no hot bulbs, vapourisers or ignition gear'. The illustration depicts the engine as a generating package. (Authors' collection)

The second submarine to be completed by White's in the First World War was the *F2*, seen here. With a displacement of 353 tons and a length of 150ft, it was constructed in the same temporary shed on the East Cowes side of the river in which the *E32* had been built. (Royal Naval Submarine Museum)

When the Admiralty's preference for bomber aircraft changed in favour of multi-engined types, fifteen of the Wight Landplane Bombers on order with White's were cancelled. White's proposed that they should be completed instead as float planes, to which the Admiralty agreed. Thus, the Wight Converted Seaplane, the AD Type N2b, came into being. A total of forty were built, beginning with the delivery of the first machine in 1917. They were distinguished by their wing-tip floats. (J. Samuel White Archives)

As the conflict at sea became more tactical, White's met a new challenge by supplying the Admiralty with four 'Q'-ships designated *PC71–PC74* (yard Nos 1508–1511). This photo shows *PC74*. She gives the appearance, intentionally, of an innocuous emergency-built cargo ship but her function was that of a decoy to draw U-boats to within the range of a seemingly defenceless merchant ship, whereby she would overwhelm them by her rapid shell fire. (Maritime Photo Library)

HMS *Vortigen* (yard No.1492) was launched by White's on 15 October 1917. She was the third of five 312ft-long 'V/W'-class destroyers to be completed by the yard. These destroyers were among the first to have single reduction gearing thus cutting down propeller revolutions and the risk of cavitation. Their high boiler pressure of 250 psi enabled them to achieve a speed of 37–38 knots driven by twin screws. In 1916 the Royal Navy took the bold step with the 'V/W'-class of shipping two guns forward and aft and superimposing the inner pair over the outer guns. This disposition had not been extended to destroyers earlier as there was concern that the additional top weight could impair stability. For the next thirty years this arrangement remained the standard layout of destroyer design. (J. Samuel White Archives)

Among the final destroyers built by the company in the First World War were seven 'Modified W'-class destroyers. An eighth vessel was cancelled. In this impressive bow quarter view, taken at sea level, HMS *Wolverine* (yard No.1494), is seen at speed on trials. Delivered in July 1920, the *Wolverine* survived to perform war service for a second time nineteen years later. In total, eight White's-built First World War destroyers saw service in the second war, including the already seen *Vortigern*, the majority of them as short or long-range convoy escorts. The *Wolverine* was scrapped at Troon in September 1946, ending a twenty-six-year career. (J. Samuel White Archives)

During 1918, besides other warships being built, five 'S'-class destroyers were launched. These were built to Admiralty specifications and were smaller, faster and quicker to build than the 'V's and 'W's. New features included in them were the rounded sides to the forecastle deck and a pair of fixed 14in torpedo tubes mounted just aft of the break of the forecastle deck. This image of HMS *Truant* (yard No.1513), showing her underway when later based at Devonport, reveals some of the aforementioned new modifications. She was completed on 17 March 1919, after the Armistice, so did not see war service. (Authors' collection)

PART THREE

1918-39

The yard's tally of warship production towards the war effort had been impressive. However, with the return of peace the major orders from the Admiralty ceased. The war with Germany was over but the battle for yard survival was about to begin. In 1919, throughout the UK's shipbuilding industry the working week was reduced from fifty-four hours to forty-seven hours; in 1920 there were over 350,000 workers employed in the industry nationally. That same year White's were completing four out of five destroyers launched after the Armistice but a further four on order were cancelled, progress on construction was halted and any incomplete structures dismantled.

A new era had arrived in the industry whereby contracts were placed on a cash basis and the price paid to the shipbuilder by instalments. These could vary to some extent but were normally paid at contract signing, on keel laying, on completion of framing, on completion of plating, at launch and on delivery.

Owing to the post-war recession and lack of orders in the industry many small shipyards throughout the land were either closed permanently or closed and reopened later as the market picked up. Between 1920 and 1926 only eight destroyers were ordered by the Admiralty; none of these orders were placed with White's. However, the firm was sustained by orders from the most unlikely sources, mainly for commercial vessels such as Great Lakes steamers, launches, barges, colliers, ferries and tugs. During this post-war period, orders for lifeboats from the Royal National Lifeboat Institution flourished, and it seemed ironical that the company, instead of building warships that destroyed other vessels and lives, was now concentrating on vessels that saved lives.

In 1924 a challenging contract from the Greek Government was taken on to overhaul and completely rebuild the destroyers *Ierax*, *Leon*, *Aetos*, and *Panther*. The following year saw the completion of the large paddle passenger steamer *Crested Eagle* for the General Steam Navigation Co. Around this time, the company opened a Repair Department, auspiciously located within the Old Docks at Southampton.

By 1928, a much-needed order arrived in the form of three flotilla leader destroyers, the *Mendoza*, *Tucuman* and *La Rioja* for the Argentine Navy, all completed in 1929. Their delivery coincided with the Wall Street Crash of that year and the ensuing global Depression. Again, many smaller shipyards closed during this time, but White's fared better than most. Indeed, many shipyard workers from the Tyne and Wear yards migrated south in the hope that they could secure work at White's. By 1930, small orders such as for the private yachts *Braemar* (1 and 2) and the *Xarifa* (1 and 2) along with naval pinnaces kept the yard ticking over; then, for the first time since the Armistice, the Admiralty placed an order, for a 'C'-class destroyer, HMS *Kempenfelt*. It seemed that the 'boat had come in', albeit temporarily. This was followed in 1933 by an order for two 'F'-class destroyers, *Forester* and *Fury*, for the Royal Navy.

The General Election of 1935 returned a Conservative Government to power who were committed to a policy of rearmament. This was as a direct result of the rapid expansion that had taken place in the German, Italian and Japanese navies. This policy manifested itself in increased numbers of new warship orders.

For White's, the year 1935 proved something of a watershed, when the order for two smaller warships known as sloops was placed by the Admiralty simultaneous with the receipt of the prestigious contract for the Polish Navy destroyers *Grom* and *Blyskawica*, which were to be the largest in the world when they entered service. By this time the world financial situation was beginning to improve and between 1935 and the outbreak of the Second World War in September 1939, White's launched a further six destroyers and two more sloops for the Admiralty. Over the period between the wars, the company had actually constructed some 348 vessels of various types, which included eighty-four lifeboats for the RNLI. But the war clouds were gathering...

Following the Armistice and a rapid decline in warship production, a series of valuable post-war commercial orders materialised. These were for six steel colliers for foreign and British owners. They were the *Argonne* and *Auvergne*, pictured above, (yard Nos 1544 and 1549) for the Compania Delmas of France, the *Bilton*, *River Wear* and *River Tees* (yard Nos 1545–1547) for Lythgoe Prince Ship Management and the *Atlas* (yard No.1548) for the Norwegian whaling company A/S Atlas (Jacobsen & Co.). All were delivered during 1920. (World Ship Society)

This is the *Atlas* (yard No.1548), delivered to Jacobsen & Co., Langesund, Norway. Renamed *Aintree* in 1922 and *Folda* three years later, after transfer to Christian Salvesen Co., Edinburgh, she was broken up at Rosyth in 1956. (Wayne Pritchett)

At the southern end of the West Cowes shipyard are three 125ft oil barges completed in 1921 for the British Oil Bunkering Co., namely the *Perso*, *Pando* and *Poilo* (yard Nos 1556–1558), along with other craft. A year later three similar-sized spirit barges were completed for the British Tanker Company. (Keith MacDonald)

The Norwegian-flag cargo ship *Leka* of C.T. Gogstad & Co., Oslo, was built by White's as the *Hitherwood* (yard No.1562) for C.A. Stewart & Co., London. As the *Leka* she performed stalwart wartime duties running the gauntlet of German S-boats and warplanes as she made numerous coastwise convoy voyages delivering essential supplies around the UK. Her travels took her to Welsh, south coast and north east ports and, on nine occasions, she visited The Solent, discharging off Cowes, her birthplace. (World Ship Society)

One of the initial pair of specialised paddle ferries completed for the London County Council for the Thames crossing at Woolwich was the 625 gross ton *Squires* (yard No.1589) built at a cost of £69,290. She maintained the service with three other White's-built sisters until October 1963 when she was sold for breaking up at Bruges. They had White's-built diagonal steam reciprocating engines driving paddles. The boilers were coke-fired and manually stoked to reduce excessive smoke and, worked at a pressure of 60 psi, they consumed eight tons of fuel a day. At 171ft 6in in length between perpendiculars and 62ft wide over their paddle sponsons, they were capable of carrying 100 passengers on the main deck and 90 tons of vehicles on the deck above. (Kenneth W. Wightman)

▲ As the only ships of the type built by White's, the Great Lakes steamers *Judge Hart* and *Norman P. Clements* (yard Nos 1599 and 1600) were completed for the Eastern Steamship Co. The picture shows the *Norman P. Clements* which blew up at Collingwood, Ontario, on 16 October 1968 and was scuttled. (Beken of Cowes)

◄ This White's advert shows that the company had rapidly diversified into the vast field of marine engineering production. Taking one product in isolation, the two-cylinder, semi-diesel 'Super' model, it should be remembered that the oil engine was then still in its infancy. A semi-diesel was one in which the diesel fuel was sprayed into a hot bulb chamber with previously compressed air such that ignition took place in the chamber before passing into the main cylinder. This ensured that pressure was maintained in the cylinder and all injected fuel was completely burned. (Authors' collection)

Launched in March 1925, the *Crested Eagle* (yard No.621) was a fast paddler of 18.75 knots with a capacity for 1,700 passengers, built for the General Steam Navigation Co. for its River Thames's services to Kent and Essex resorts. She was 1,110 gross tons and 309ft long and her triple expansion diagonal engines were oil-fired. In addition she was fitted with a telescopic funnel and a hinged mast to enable her to pass under London's bridges. The *Crested Eagle* is thought to have been the second largest coastal excursion paddle steamer built in the UK during the twentieth century, exceeded only by her fleet-mate *Royal Eagle*. (General Steam Navigation Co.; courtesy of Isle of Wight Heritage Service)

Built originally from an order of four destroyers for the Argentine Government by Cammell Laird of Birkenhead but, as their speed failed to meet the contractual requirement of 35 knots, they were rejected. As such, they were taken up by the Greek Government in 1911 and named *Aetos, Panther, Ierax* and *Leon*. The *Panther* was the ex-*Santiago* and the *Leon* the ex-*Tucuman*. Thirteen years later they were modernised by White's. The photograph shows the *Leon* as it arrived at Cowes to commence refurbishment. (Kirk; courtesy of Isle of Wight Heritage Service)

White's completed the modernisation of the multi-funnelled Greek destroyers *Actos, Panther, Ierax* and *Leon* in 1924, a contract that was worth £500,000. This is the rebuilt *Panther* (yard No.1617). Along with the *Aetos* and *Ierax*, the *Panther* escaped from Greece in April 1941 to join Allied naval forces based at Alexandria. (J. Samuel White Archives)

Another view of the affectionately regarded paddle steamer *Crested Eagle* (yard No.1621). She was taken up by the Admiralty as an auxiliary anti-aircraft vessel on the outbreak of the Second World War and whilst in this role she was sunk during the evacuation of the British Expeditionary Force from Dunkirk, bombed on 29 May 1940 with the loss of over 300 lives. (Alex Duncan)

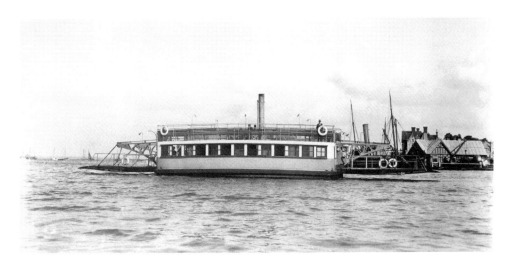

In 1924, White's were contracted to build two similar steam-driven chain ferries or floating bridges. Both were delivered in 1925. This is *Floating Bridge No.2* (yard No.1627), a 48ft craft for Cowes Ferry Commission, for use on the Cowes and East Cowes link across the River Medina. She remained on the Medina crossing for only ten years, sold in 1936 when *Floating Bridge No.3* entered service, then joining the White's-built *Poole Ferry No.1* on the Sandbanks to Studland service. (Kirk; courtesy of Isle of Wight Heritage Service)

A cargo steamer completed for the General Steam Navigation Co. in October 1925 was the 890 gross ton *Fauvette* (yard No.1631). She was lost in a collision between Dunkirk and Ostend on 26 February 1934. (Tom Rayner)

The company's long association with the Crown Agents for the Colonies and the India Office led to further orders for river craft and ferries. One of them was the *Audrey* (yard No.1643), a 128ft ferry delivered in 1927 intended for service at Lagos in Nigeria. Unlike previous stern-wheeler river craft that White's had built for the Crown Agents, the *Audrey* was screw driven. (Kirk; courtesy of Isle of Wight Heritage Service)

The elegant paddle ferry *Freshwater* (yard No.1645) was built for the Southern Railway to maintain the passenger service between Lymington, Hampshire, and Yarmouth, Isle of Wight, in which she entered in May 1927. She continued in operation on the crossing until 1962 when she was sold for excursion service and renamed *Swanage Queen*. (Tom Rayner)

The second *Xarifa* (yard No.1646), designed by J.M. Soper and built for Mr F. Mortimer Singer, was delivered in 1927. This view shows the 269 tons displacement, 118ft, three-masted auxiliary schooner in full sail off Cowes, flying the owner's US Ensign. In 1951, the second *Xarifa* was bought by voyager and underwater researcher Hans Hass and in his ownership she sailed extensively in the Pacific and Indian Oceans. At the time of writing this vessel is still in active service based in Monte Carlo available for charter, conferences and hospitality events. (Kirk; courtesy of Isle of Wight Heritage Service)

A striking auxiliary steam yacht built for the Straits Settlement Government, Singapore, was the 844 gross ton *Sea Belle II* (yard No.1647). In this view she is seen completing at East Cowes, following her launch which took place on 13 October 1927. The *Sea Belle II* served as an auxiliary yacht during the Second World War. (Kirk; courtesy of Isle of Wight Heritage Service)

An unusual vessel that put in at White's for repairs was the Royal Research Ship *William Scoresby*. She had originally been built by Cook, Welton & Gemmell of Beverley in Yorkshire and was completed on 26 June 1926, destined for Antarctic waters. She was fitted with triple-expansion reciprocating steam engines by Amos & Smith of Hull. Repairs at White's took place during 1927 and in this picture she is seen moored alongside at Cowes. (Kirk; courtesy of Keith MacDonald)

Apart from orders for new construction during the 1920s, White's was also contracted to undertake a range of conversion tasks, in some cases modifying naval craft surplus to requirements after the First World War for commercial trading. In other cases, it involved engine adaptation from coal to oil burning as in the case of the Norwegian whalers *Rokk* and *Fjord* shown here, work that was completed in 1927. (Kirk; courtesy of Isle of Wight Heritage Service)

In the late 1920s the Argentine Government placed an order for three flotilla leader destroyers from the yard, the *Mendoza*, *Tucuman* and *La Rioja* (yard Nos 1651–1653). The first of these, the *Mendoza*, was launched on 16 October 1928. This photo shows one of the 'Mendoza'-class in the River Medina approaching another that is moored alongside the fitting-out quay. (Chris Bancroft)

▲ The major order for three modern destroyers for the Argentine Navy represented the resumption of naval construction at White's in the period between the wars. First to be completed for delivery in June 1929 was the *Mendoza* (yard No.1651), name-ship of the class, shown here on speed trials. Apart from the 'Broke'-class ships, built fifteen years earlier, they were the largest naval vessels so far built by the shipyard at 1,570 displacement tons and with an overall length of 321ft 3in, they were also marginally the longest destroyers thus far built by White's. (Kirk; courtesy of Isle of Wight Heritage Service)

▼ One of the 'Mendoza'-class destroyers is seen here under tow in the River Medina *c*.1930, possibly the *La Rioja* (yard No.1653). The three ships served the Argentine Navy until they were paid off for disposal in April 1962. (Authors' collection)

This photograph shows a pair of boilers, Nos 68 and 69, completed by the Engineering and Boiler-Making Department for the Metropolitan Water Board. Concealed within their casings, the company's nameplate can be seen mounted on the front of each unit, below the pressure gauges. They are fitted with Bennis Automated, Patent Chain Grate Stokers, fabricated at that company's works at Little Hulton, near Bolton, the chute of each clearly seen at the front. (Isle of Wight Heritage Service)

The fourth and last built of the Woolwich free ferry quartet was the *John Benn* (yard No.1685), named after Sir John Benn (1858–1922), a relative of Anthony Wedgewood Benn, the former Labour MP. Instead of protruding sponsons as was normally found on paddle steamers, the *John Benn* and the others of her type had their paddle boxes integral with the main hull structure. (Pamlin Prints)

Fortunately for the White's workforce the second *Xarifa* did not remain long in Mr Franklin Mortimer Singer's ownership and he ordered a third *Xarifa* (yard No.1686), a twin-screwed steam yacht with a distinctive spoon-shaped bow form, that was launched from the Falcon Yard on 13 May 1930, minus her masts and funnel. Unlike the two earlier *Xarifas* built by White's, the third of the name was solely steam-powered and did not carry auxiliary sails. (Wayne Pritchett)

The third *Xarifa* (yard No.1686), which measured 731 gross tons and 204ft 4in in length overall, was one of the last big steam yachts to be built in the UK. She was powered by two triple expansion steam reciprocating engines. She remained in Mr Singer's ownership from 1930–47 but was taken over for auxiliary service with the Royal Navy during the Second World War as HMS *Black Bear*. After the war, she was bought for commercial interests and renamed S/Y *Cymania*. (Kirk; courtesy of Isle of Wight Heritage Service)

J. SAMUEL WHITE & CO. LTD.,

SHIPBUILDERS AND ENGINEERS,

EAST COWES, I.O.W.

TELEGRAMS: "WHITE, EAST COWES."   TELEPHONE NO. 3 COWES (3 lines).

BUILDERS OF FAST PASSENGER AND CARGO STEAMERS.
SPECIAL SERVICE AND SHALLOW-DRAUGHT VESSELS.
TORPEDO BOAT DESTROYERS.
STEAM AND MOTOR LAUNCHES OF EVERY CLASS.

MANUFACTURERS OF MARINE STEAM TURBINES, RECIPROCATING MACHINERY.
" WHITE-FORSTER " WATER TUBE BOILERS, MARINE RETURN TUBE BOILERS.
" J. SAMUEL WHITE " OIL FUEL BURNING INSTALLATION.
" J. SAMUEL WHITE " SUPER SEMI DIESEL ENGINES.

LONDON
28, Victoria Street, Westminster, S.W. 1.

LIVERPOOL
707-711, Royal Liver Building.

A White's shipyard advertisement from the *Journal of Commerce Annual Review* of 1925. (Authors' collection)

White's opened a Repair Department within Southampton's Old Docks in the years immediately following the First World War, a valuable supplement to the company's business on the Island here photographed from the air in December 1926. The facility, manned with skilled staff, comprised workshops conveniently close to the Prince of Wales dry dock, the latter used to carry out work on the underwater hulls of vessels recently launched at Cowes, such as cleaning, painting and removal of drag gear. (Isle of Wight Heritage Service)

White's built several lightships for overseas customers, most notably the Calcutta Port Trust. The only craft of this type built for the Corporation of Trinity House was No.86 (yard No.1701), delivered to the Edinburgh station. Later, she was transferred to Cork and finally the Nore, the oldest lightship station in the world, established in the 1700s. Now owned privately, she is currently located at Port Wexburgh Marina, Hoo, Rochester, where she is undergoing preservation. (Authors' collection)

The first destroyer order received from the Admiralty since the Armistice was for HMS *Kempenfelt* (yard No.1707), a 'C' or 'Crusader'-class flotilla leader destroyer, launched on 29 February 1931. At 1,375 tons displacement, 318ft in length and a speed of 36 knots, she was a development of the 'Mendoza'-class and a precursor to HMS *Forester* and *Fury*. She was armed with four 4.7in guns and eight torpedo tubes. Transferred to the Royal Canadian Navy from October 1939 and renamed HMCS *Assiniboine*, whilst on escort duty on 6 August 1942 she rammed and sunk the German submarine *U-210*. (Authors' collection)

▲ A second, twin-screw steel motor yacht, named *Braemar* (yard No.1725), was launched by White's for Captain George Paxton and delivered in June 1931. She was constructed of galvanised 8mm steel (the same as used on warships) with five watertight bulkheads, and displaced 182 tons on a length of 123ft. Driven by two 255 hp MAN engines she could achieve a speed of 13 knots. (Kirk; courtesy of Isle of Wight Heritage Service)

▼ Trials with self-righting lifeboats built by the company were carried out prior to delivery at the Shepard Brothers wharf in West Cowes. Here the *Herbert Joy II* (yard No.1710) can be seen undergoing a righting test in June 1931 before she was delivered to the Scarborough station. (Authors' collection)

▲ During the Second World War, the *Braemar*, seen here completed, served as the British armed yacht *Clorinde*. Re-engined in the 1950s, she was renamed *Meltemi* between 1981 and 1983 and more recently became the *Amphora*. At the time of writing she remains in active operation, privately-owned, now more than 80 years from when she was completed. (Kirk; courtesy of Isle of Wight Heritage Service)

Walmer Lifeboat and Crew.

▲ The 40ft, self-righting lifeboat *Civil Service No.4* was delivered on 10 August 1932, destined for the Whitehills (Walmer) Lifeboat Station where she is seen beached. Funds to finance and sponsor the Civil Service lifeboats were raised from the Civil Service Sports Association members' contributions. This vessel served on station through to 1948. (Isle of Wight Heritage Service)

◄ This is HMS *Fury* (yard No.1752), of the 'F' or 'Fearless'-class, sister ship of HMS *Forester* (yard No.1751). Launched on 10 September 1934 she was delivered in May 1935. The armament on these ships was similar to that of HMS *Kempenfelt* and they were of comparable size, displacing 1,350 tons with a length of 318ft 3in. Their turbines developed 34,000 shp giving them a speed of 36.5 knots. Their radius of action at 15 knots was around 6,000 miles. (Maritime Photo Library)

As a private constructor, White's built a record number of lifeboats for the RNLI, including examples of most of the types introduced by the service, a magnificent total of 134 boats. This is the *Joseph Braithwaite* (yard No.1772), a 36ft 'Liverpool'-class boat. She was delivered on 28 August 1934 to the Maryport station. (Beken of Cowes)

White's only built eleven tugs, the first being the steam-powered *Nancy* (yard No.1181) delivered to Risdale & Wells in 1903. This is the 60ft motor tug *Kelpy* (yard No.1777), the first of four such craft built for J.P. Knight (London) Ltd of Rochester, Kent. *Kelpy* was delivered in October 1934. (Authors' collection)

Another firefloat constructed for the London County Council was the *Massey Shaw* (yard No.1778), here seen being launched from the slipway in East Cowes on 25 February 1935. Vessels like the *Massey Shaw* were to demonstrate their full value during the Blitz on London's dockland, a prime target for the Luftwaffe. Prior to that, she served with distinction during the evacuation of Dunkirk, exploiting her shallow draught to get right inshore. Her entire crew received a commendation for their contribution. (Isle of Wight Heritage Service)

The firefloat *Massey Shaw* (yard No.1778) seen in action fighting a warehouse fire. (London Fire Brigade)

Seen at various stages of completion in the former aircraft workshop, West Cowes, which became a dedicated boat-building shop after the First World War, are the *Rosabella* (yard No.1790), a surf-motor type, and the *WRA* (yard No.1803) and *Margaret Dawson* (yard No.1804), both 'Liverpool'-type boats. The *Rosabella* went to the Ilfracombe station. The *WRA* and *Margaret Dawson* were stationed respectively at North Sunderland and Gourdon. (Fox; courtesy of Isle of Wight Heritage Service)

In 1930 the first London Naval Treaty defined a 'sloop' as a vessel not exceeding a displacement of 2,000 tons, capable of a speed not greater than 20 knots, and with an armament of only four 6in guns and no torpedo tubes. Two such vessels were ordered from White's, HMS *Niger*, seen here on trials, and *Salamander* (yard Nos 1791 and 1792) both 'Halcyon'-class sloop-minesweepers. Though initially built for minesweeping, they would be the precursor for specialised convoy escorts. Launched on 29 January 1936, the *Niger* was approximately 800 tons displacement and 230ft long, with two 4in and one 3in AA guns. Her speed was 17 knots and she had a crew of eighty. (J. Samuel White Archives)

The launch of ORP *Blyskawica* (yard No.1801) on 1 October 1936 for the Polish Navy. To the top of the picture, beyond the tug, is the ORP *Grom* (yard No.1800). She had been temporarily moved clear while her sister was being launched. At 2,140 tons displacement and 377ft long overall, these two Polish destroyers were the largest destroyers so far constructed by the yard and among the largest destroyers in the world at that time. (Wayne Pritchett)

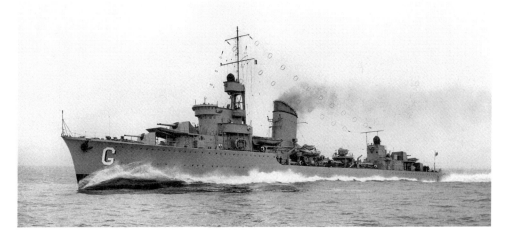

The move to the one-funnel destroyer design in the *Grom* and *Blyskawica* pre-empted the Admiralty. Capable of achieving 39 knots, the *Grom* and her sister were initially armed with seven 4.7in, four 3in AA guns and six triple-torpedo tubes. The *Grom* and the *Blyskawica* were also equipped for mine laying and their hulls were strengthened for ice navigation. This view shows the *Grom* at full speed during her trials. (Beken of Cowes)

Along with the *Minnehaha* (yard No.1819), also built by White's, the *Noneta* (yard No.1802) completed in 1935 is another of the few surviving 'Little Ships' that assisted in the evacuation of Dunkirk in June 1940. Her engines, as built, were twin Gardner diesels. Still afloat, latterly she was Maltese flagged and available for charter in the Western Mediterranean, marketed as 'the perfect Gentlemen's boat'. However, at the time of writing she was up for sale at La Coruña in Spain. One of her attractive original features was her 'Bremen' bow, still retained. (Beken of Cowes)

HMS *Intrepid* (yard No.1811) the lead ship of the 'I' or 'Intrepid'-class on builder's trials. At her stern the flag 'White's-Cowes' may be clearly seen, a modification on the earlier 'W' house flag. She was 312ft long and armed with four 4.7in guns and eight torpedo tubes. Her twin-shaft steam turbines produced 34,000 shp which gave her a speed of 36.5 knots. Capable of carrying a crew of 145, she had a radius of action of 6.000 miles at 15 knots cruising speed. Her sister was the *Impulsive* (yard No.1812), completed in July 1937. (Maritime Photo Library)

Floating Bridge No. 3 (yard No.1813) was the second chain ferry to be built by White's to the order of the Cowes Urban District Council and the first ferry on the Cowes–East Cowes service to have diesel-electric propulsion. Seen here in the River Medina on the occasion of her launch, *Floating Bridge No. 3* had distinctive stairway enclosures leading to the upper deck passenger spaces. Following a period of relief during winter overhauls after *Floating Bridge No. 4* was commissioned in 1952, *Floating Bridge No. 3* was sold for breaking up but sank in The Solent in 1975 while under tow to Southampton. (Kirk; courtesy of Isle of Wight Heritage Service)

J.P. Knight (London) Ltd awarded a follow-on order to the motor tug *Kelpy* (yard No.1777), built by White's in 1934, for the similar-sized *Kathleen* and *Katra* (yard Nos 1814 and 1815) both delivered in 1936. The *Katra*, seen here, the second of the pair to be built, was launched on 29 January 1936. She measured 68 gross tons and was 67ft long and diesel driven, her engines producing 520 bhp. She was scrapped in 1984. (World Ship Society)

◄ HMS *Bittern* (yard No.1820) was launched on 14 July 1937, the lead Convoy Escort Sloop of the 'Bittern'-class. She was the third sloop ordered from White's just prior to the Second World War and at 1,190 displacement tons and 266ft length was slightly larger than the *Niger* and *Salamander*. Also that year she was re-designated as an escort vessel. Ironically this picture of the launch was taken by a German photographer; clearly Britain's expanding naval capability was of great interest to the Third Reich High Command at that time. (David Hutchings)

▼ The convoy escort vessel HMS *Egret* (yard No.1835) takes to the water on 31 May 1938, with the tug *Hector* standing by in the foreground. She was a modified version of the *Bittern*, having a displacement tonnage of 1,200 and an increased length of 276ft. She mounted eight 4in guns, all of which could be used as AA weapons. On 27 August 1943 the *Egret* was hit by a German glider bomb off north-west Spain. She sank with the loss of 194 of her crew. (Kirk; courtesy of Isle of Wight Heritage Service)

▲   The completed escort sloop HMS *Bittern* (yard No.1820) photographed on builder's trials prior to delivery to the Royal Navy in March 1938. She was armed with three 4in guns which could also be used as AA weapons but she became one of the first casualties of the war when she was bombed by a German Heinkel on 30 April 1940 while lying in Namsos Fjord. (Kirk; courtesy of J. Samuel White Archives)

▼   White's embarked on a most enterprising project in the late 1930s, testifying to the company's enduring reputation as an innovative constructor. This was the construction of the 67ft by 14ft 6in aluminium-hulled Motor Torpedo Boat 101 (yard No.1824) built as a private venture experimental craft, though with Admiralty interest from the outset. She was fitted with hydrofoils, a unique feature for this type of vessel, making her something of a missing link in the development of dynamic lift planing craft. Fitted with three Isotta Fraschini petrol engines, the best speed achieved on trials after MTB 101 was completed in 1939 was 42 knots. The Admiralty acquired MTB 101 for £51,000 and continued to put it through its paces until 16 November 1940. Whereas hydrofoils offered the operational advantage of rapid acceleration from rest or low speed, the foils and stern gear of these craft were extremely vulnerable to damage, especially during the intensive employment and frequent docking that was typical of wartime operation. Ultimately, this was to prove MTB 101's Achilles' heel, for she was lost in 1942 when damage to one of her foils caused the struts to collapse. (Beken of Cowes)

The last pair of destroyers constructed to the order of the Admiralty prior to the outbreak of the Second World War were the similar 'Javelin'-class *Jersey* (yard No.1837), seen here, and Kelly-class *Kingston* (yard No.1838). They were the first modern-looking, single-funnel destroyers to be completed for the Royal Navy by White's. In fact, the 'J'-class ships were the first single-funnel destroyers since 1895. Launched on 26 September 1938, *Jersey* was delivered in April 1939 only to become a war casualty on 2 May 1941 after striking a mine off the entrance to Grand Harbour, Valletta. (Maritime Photo Library)

Two destroyers originally ordered for the Brazilian Navy as the *Javary* and *Jutaby* (yard Nos 1868 and 1869), were launched on 17 July and 16 October 1939 respectively but owing to the outbreak of the Second World War they were commandeered by the Admiralty and renamed HMS *Havant* and *Havelock*. At 1,340 tons displacement and 312ft long they were based on the earlier 'H' or 'Hero'-class design. This image shows HMS *Havant*. She was bombed and sunk on 1 June 1940 whilst assisting in the Dunkirk evacuation. (Crown Copyright)

PART FOUR

1939-45

As in the First World War, White's once again geared up for maximum output of ships and engines following the outbreak of renewed hostilities with Germany in September 1939, immediately implementing a rotating shift system to permit construction around the clock. Already, even before the war had started, the company had been contracted to build a number of new warships and effort during the first year of the conflict was concentrated on completing and delivering these vessels. In so doing White's added to the significant achievements it could already claim.

Recognising the need to arrange naval construction most efficiently in order to maximise production output from the nation's shipyards, White's was designated as a destroyer builder and the orders for other naval vessels that had not been started were cancelled.

Repair and overhaul work on destroyers was to be another mainstay of the shipyard's wartime effort and it included, fortuitously, the Polish Navy's ORP *Blyskawica* which was alongside at Cowes when the Luftwaffe carried out its heaviest air raid on the town in May 1942, dropping 200 tons of high explosives and incendiaries. The ship's guns were central to the relentless anti-aircraft barrage that drove off the marauding bombers.

Among the notable warships completed by White's during the war years was the fast minelayer HMS *Abdiel*, the longest ship ever built at the yard. Launched from a slipway that was almost 50ft shorter than the ship itself, it was said that her bow projected above the workshops alongside Clarence Road while her stern stuck out into the river. On launch day, 23 April 1940, the tugs on standby had to be especially nifty to arrest the hull's momentum in a space that was barely wider than the ship was long.

Another one-off was the steam gunboat HMS *Grey Goose*, a small but powerful craft conceived as a miniature destroyer. Fitted with powerful steam turbines for quiet running and high speed, she was used along with others of her class for secretive, solo blockade-breaking runs to Sweden to collect vital cargoes of ball bearings. She was commanded by the famed ornithologist, painter and naturalist Peter Scott, son of Robert Falcon Scott, the Antarctic explorer.

As a testament to White's expertise and acknowledged reputation as a first-class naval constructor, the Admiralty entrusted to the company the contract for the first ever all-welded destroyer, delivered in November 1945 as HMS *Contest*. White's had to develop and trouble-shoot the techniques of welded construction, to be adopted subsequently by other builders, and itself received orders for three more 'C'-class ships constructed by the same method.

Throughout the war, the boat shops, which from April 1939 had identified the vessels built there on a separate construction list, were kept fully occupied with Motor Torpedo Boats, Air Sea Rescue launches for the RAF, seaplane tenders, picket boats, lifeboats and sundry smaller boats, amassing a total output of 339 craft.

J. Samuel White's also retained an involvement in aircraft production throughout the Second World War, not complete machines as it had constructed earlier but vital components in support of leading aircraft manufacturers distributed around the country. Although the Aviation Department had been officially closed on 28 July 1919 and the Somerton Works disposed of in the 1920s to Selsdon Aero & Engineering Company, sometime in the intervening years White's had reacquired the workshops and launched new production lines. Already, from around 1937, all types of metal assemblies and components were being produced for Supermarine Spitfires and this was followed, as wartime aircraft construction ramped up, with parts for Avro Lancaster and de Havilland Mosquito bombers. Capable of machining and welding to fine tolerances with a range of treatments and finishes, the company produced fuselage frames, wing ribs, elevators, ailerons, controls, seat gear and undercarriage assemblies.

After the First World War, a display board had been mounted on the shipyard gates proudly listing the company's output for the war effort under the heading: 'We did our bit!' Though such a list may not have been displayed in 1945, at the end of the Second World War, nevertheless the company could rightly claim to have 'done its bit' for a second time. Representing some of the Boat Shop production outlined above and including the vessels that were under construction in the main yard on the outbreak of war, as well as those that were still incomplete at the cessation of hostilities in August 1945, there were:

One fast minelayer: *Abdiel*.

Twenty-three destroyers: *Havant, Havelock, Quorn, Southdown, Silverton* (renamed *Krakowiak*), *Puckeridge, Southwold, Tetcott, Quentin, Quiberon, Quickmatch, Easton, Eggesford, Stevenstone, Talybont, Success* (renamed *Stord*), *Swift, Vixen* (renamed *Sioux*), *Volage, Cavalier, Carysfort, Contest* and *Crispin*.

One steam gunboat: *Grey Goose*.

Thirteen landing craft: LCM 29–32, LCA 87–90, LCT 7034, LCM 123–126 and LCT 4128.

Two motor gunboats: MGB 47 and 48.

Thirty-eight motor torpedo boats: MTB 41–48, 201–212, 246–257 and 424–429.

Lead ship of her class, HMS *Abdiel* (yard No.1881), became the largest warship to be built at White's as well as the longest ship ever launched at Cowes. With an overall hull length of 418ft and a beam of 40ft, her launch on 23 April 1940 was a delicate affair with only feet to spare between the two banks of the river. Of 2,650 tons standard displacement and a full load displacement of over 4,000 tons, these ships were essentially of light cruiser size. They were built flush-decked with the main deck aft used to stow 160 mines. Here the *Abdiel* nears completion alongside the fitting-out quay at Cowes, a photograph of her probably taken around the time of her delivery in April 1941. (Carisbrooke Castle Museum)

Power for the 'Abdiel'-class minelayers was provided by two sets of geared turbines, supplied by steam at 300 psi and a temperature of 645°F from four three-drum water tube boilers, which developed 72,000 shp, giving them a speed of 39 knots (although White's unofficially recorded that she had exceeded 40 knots on one occasion!). Armament consisted of two twin 4.7in guns fore and aft. Rushed into service before she had even completed official trials, the *Abdiel* was lost on 10 September 1943 after striking a mine herself in Taranto Bay, Italy, with the loss of forty-eight of her crew and 120 troops. (Crown Copyright)

Although White's wartime output from the main shipyard was focused on destroyer construction, a great variety of other military craft was produced in the boat shop, among them two three-screw Motor Gun Boats, one of which was MGB 47 (yard No.5016) delivered in August 1940. Conceived as Motor Anti-Submarine Boats for the Polish Navy, she had Isotta Fraschini petrol engines with a total bhp of 3,450 giving her a top speed of 42 knots. Requisitioned by the Royal Navy, they were completed as MGBs, the only two of this type of craft built by White's. (Isle of Wight Heritage Service)

Although the major suppliers of MTBs were Vospers and the British Powerboat Company, White's gained a small share of the wartime orders for coastal forces craft. This image shows the MTB 41 (yard No.5045), the first of a group of eight boats, MTBs 41 to 48, at speed in calm waters. They were powered by Stirling Admiral petrol engines with a large fuel storage. (Isle of Wight Heritage Service)

Among the destroyers completed during the Second World War were ten 'Hunt'-class escorts. The 'Hunt' Type II *Silverton* (yard No.1899), launched on 4 December 1940, was delivered to the Free Polish Navy as the *Krakowiak* in May 1941, as seen here. Returned to the Royal Navy in 1946, the *Silverton* was broken up at Grays, Essex, from March 1959. (Marek Twardowski)

The 'Q'-class destroyer *Quickmatch* (yard No.1909) of 1,705 tons displacement and 359ft overall length was launched on 11 April 1942 and commissioned into naval service that September. She was transferred to the Royal Australian Navy in December 1942 and served in the Pacific along with her White's-built sister *Quiberon*, latterly performing sweeps of the Japanese coast in the closing months of the war, and bombarding the Tokyo area. (Maritime Photo Library)

▲ A 'Hunt'-class Type III destroyer, one of four completed by the company in just over a year, HMS *Eggesford* (yard No.1917) was launched on 12 September 1942. The Type III, measuring 1,087 displacement tons, had an increased beam of 31ft 6in compared with the earlier Type I batch, giving them improved stability. They were also equipped with twin torpedo tubes. Though of limited range, these escort destroyers were manoeuvrable and fast with quick acceleration, ideal for anti-submarine duties. (Maritime Photo Library)

▼ One of seven craft of a type built to a Denny hybrid design, somewhere between a full-size destroyer and an MGB, was the steam-powered gun boat *Grey Goose* (yard No.1920), also known as SGB 9. Unsuitable for combat duties because of the vulnerability of their steam plant to small-calibre gunfire, these boats were stripped down as their high speed and quiet running suited them to another purpose, as blockade runners fetching essential machined parts from Sweden. Adapted as a test bed for gas turbine propulsion after the Second World War, the *Grey Goose* survives today as the house boat *Anserava* at Hoo, Kent. (Crown Copyright)

Berthed alongside the shipyard's West Cowes fitting-out quay is the Polish super-destroyer *Blyskawica*, seen nearing completion. Five years later, while berthed in the exact same position, the *Blyskawica*, drawing power from ashore, deployed her guns to great effect, maintaining an intensive aerial barrage that prevented German warplanes from carrying out the total destruction of the town. (Authors' collection)

Another of the total of thirty-two White's type MTBs built for the Royal Navy, MTB 252 was one of six craft (yard Nos 5205–5210) ordered for HMS *Hornet* in 1942 and delivered during the second half of 1943. Like the craft of the previous series, MTBs 252–257 had Stirling petrol engines driving three shafts, giving them a speed of 40 knots. (Crown Copyright; courtesy of Keith MacDonald)

The 'S'-class destroyer *Success* (yard No.1921), launched on 3 April 1943, was transferred under the command of the Free Norwegian naval force on delivery in September 1943 and, as such, she was renamed *Stord*. She was one of two ships of this class built by White's, both intended for the 5th Emergency Flotilla, the other being HMS *Swift* which remained with the Royal Navy. They had a displacement of 1,796 tons and their overall length was 339ft 6in. (Beken of Cowes)

The emergency destroyers HMS *Vixen* and *Volage* (yard Nos 1923 and 1924) of the 'V'-class were launched on 14 September and 15 December 1943 respectively, the latter shown here with pennant number R41. As on the smaller 'Hunt'-class ships, these destroyers had the officers' accommodation arranged forward, as this position had been found of great benefit when under combat conditions and it subsequently became standard practice for all destroyers. The *Volage* survived the war to be converted to a frigate for anti-submarine duties (see page 146). (Michael Cassar)

The first of a further group of three emergency 'Ca' or 'Caesar'-class destroyers ordered from White's was HMS *Cavalier* (yard No.1928). Originally intended to have the name *Pellew*, she was launched on 7 April 1944. Following post-war modernisation, on 6 July 1971, HMS *Cavalier* raced HMS *Rapid* over a distance of some 74 miles in the North Sea. Although the race was neck and neck most of the way, the *Cavalier* won by some 16 yards making her 'the fastest ship in the Royal Navy'. (Crown Copyright)

Second of the 'Ca'-class destroyers built by White's was HMS *Carysfort* (yard No.1929). The name *Pique* had been originally allocated to the ship. Launched on 25 July 1944, the *Carysfort* entered service on 20 February 1945, joining the Home Fleet. Subsequently, she was transferred to the East Indies station for the closing phase of the Pacific war. She remained in Royal Navy service until November 1970 when she was sold for breaking up at Newport, Wales. The photograph shows her post-war during a visit to Valletta, Malta. (Michael Cassar)

In 1943 a further group of six larger MTBs were ordered, numbers 424–429 (yard Nos 5308–5313). Though ordered by Poland, MTB 426, in this photograph, and her class-mates were first delivered to the Royal Navy in 1944 but were handed over to the Polish Navy and reassigned pennant numbers MTB S-5 to S-10. They were of 39 tons full load displacement and 75ft length. Although originally intended to have three Isotta-Fraschini petrol engines, they were fitted instead with Packards which gave them a maximum speed of 40 knots. (Isle of Wight Heritage Service)

One of the six Motor Torpedo Boats supplied to the Polish Navy during the war, this is the S-10 (yard No. 5313), ex-Royal Navy MTB 429. Despite the group being well armed with 2in rockets mounted next to the 6-pounder gun forward, two 18in torpedoes and machine guns, they never took part in action against the enemy. At the end of the war, all six boats were returned to the Royal Navy. It is worthy of note that MTB S-7 still exists as the house boat *Thanet*. (Maciej Bochenski)

Marking a significant milestone both for the Royal Navy and for J. Samuel White & Co., HMS *Contest* (yard No.1930) was the first all-welded British destroyer. A new welding shop was opened specially in East Cowes capable of handling the large sub-assemblies that were prefabricated prior to transfer to the slipway. White's did not abandon riveted construction but from that point all future naval ships were built by this method. HMS *Contest*, 2,560 tons full load displacement and 362ft 9in overall length, was launched on 16 December 1944 and commissioned on 9 November 1945. (Top: Beken of Cowes; courtesy of Carisbrooke Castle Museum; Bottom: Michael Cassar)

▼ Derived from the 'C'-class, the destroyer HMS *Scorpion* was ordered as the *Centaur*, a name subsequently allocated to a new aircraft carrier. When it was decided to build her to the specification of the larger and heavier 'Weapon'-class, she received the name *Scorpion*. Destroyers of this type had a main armament of six 4in guns plus six 40mm anti-aircraft guns and ten 21in torpedo tubes in five pairs. The class also introduced a new arrangement for the engine room layout whereby the boilers and turbines were placed in echelon formation. HMS *Scorpion* was launched on 15 August 1946 and entered service on 17 September 1947. (Michael Cassar)

▲ Once the production line had been put into place for a welding shop in which large prefabricated units could be manufactured before transference to the slipway, vessels that followed the *Contest* could be constructed in the same manner. Two such destroyers of the emergency 'Cr'-class built in this fashion were HMS *Crispin* and *Creole* (yard Nos 1931 and 1932). They were 2,560 full load displacement and 362ft 9in overall length. Although well armed, they were completed too late for the war. The welding of the thin plate of these two destroyers was less susceptible to cracking owing to greater care in welding technique and inspection. In 1956 the *Crispin* and *Creole* were transferred to the Pakistan Navy, renamed *Jahangir* and *Alamgir* respectively. (Maritime Photo Library)

Designated LCT 4128 (yard No.1939), this Mk 8 Landing Craft-Tank built to an Admiralty design, the largest and last landing craft to be built by White's, was completed by the main yard during 1945. With a length of 225ft and displacing 657 tons, LCT 4128 was driven by twin twelve-cylinder Davey, Paxman oil engines which produced 1,800bhp for a speed of 10 knots. Armament consisted of one 12-pounder and six 20mm AA guns. (Crown Copyright; courtesy of Keith MacDonald)

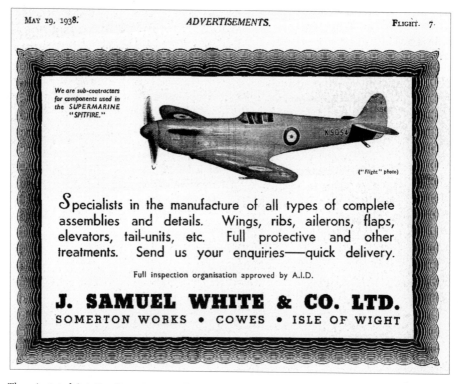

The reinstated Aviation Department at Somerton manufactured aircraft parts throughout the Second World War for bombers and fighters. This advert from 19 May 1938 promotes the company's extensive range of machined components along with a picture of the prototype Spitfire, K5054. (J. Samuel White Archives)

▶ This rather stirring advert from a 1946
*Journal of Commerce & Shipping Telegraph
Annual Review* shows a flotilla of destroyers
steaming at speed in line taken from the
bridge of a following destroyer. It cannot be
established if any were built by White's but
the purpose was to promote the company
by highlighting its envied reputation as a
destroyer builder. (Authors' collection)

▼ A general view of one of the two
boat-building shops in West Cowes that were
located towards the southern end of the
shipyard site. The shops had been intensely
busy throughout the war years and
continued to have a high level of business
over the decade that followed, with orders
for minesweepers and survey craft for the
Royal Navy and lifeboats for the RNLI. It was
during this period that White's achieved the
record which still stands today of building
more RNLI craft than any other private yard.
(J. Samuel White Archives)

The 'Daring'-class was the largest destroyer class to be built for the Royal Navy prior to 1960. Essentially a wartime design and a further development of the 'Battle' and 'Weapon'-class designs, of the eight ships ordered White's secured the contract for HMS *Dainty* (yard No.1941) on 24 January 1945. Improvements in machinery not only included two separate engine rooms but also controlled, superheat boilers and the adoption of double reduction gearing. Standard displacement was 2,830 tons, but with a full load of 3,820 she was in effect a light cruiser. This image shows HMS *Dainty* alongside at the fitting-out berth. (Authors' collection)

Another view of the destroyer HMS *Dainty* (yard No.1941). Launched on 16 August 1950, she was the last in the line of conventional destroyers which stretched back some fifty-five years to the first torpedo boat destroyer, a total of ninety-three ships since 1895. At 390ft overall length, the *Dainty* was the second-longest ship ever to be built by White's. Her main armament comprised six 4.5in guns, four 40mm AA, and a bank of quintuple torpedo tubes. A 'Squid' launcher was installed for anti-submarine warfare. (Michael Cassar)

PART FIVE

1945-66

Again, following the cessation of hostilities in 1945, all the outstanding naval orders were rapidly cancelled, thus depriving White's of five destroyer contracts. They were for the *Sword* and *Musket* of the 'Weapon'-class, the *Grafton* and *Greyhound* of the 'Gallant'-class and one of two 'Daring'-class ships, the *Dervish*. One contract remained, however, for HMS *Dainty*, one of eight large destroyers of the 'Daring'-class. She was laid down on 17 December 1945 and launched nearly five years later on 16 August 1950.

Once more the yard had to gear its expertise to building cargo ships, initially two for the French company Societé Générale de Transports Maritimes (SGTM), the yard's first ever refrigerated cargo ships, followed by two for the Argentine Government, all completed between 1947 and 1949. Also in this period there were orders for motor barges, HM Customs launches and harbour launches for the Crown Agents.

On 5 July 1951 the yard launched the fruit ship *Kadoura* for the French company Chargeurs Réunis and, on 26 February 1953, HMS *Dainty* was completed at the end of what had been a long construction period of just over seven years. Later, between 1953 and 1957, the first order placed by the Admiralty since the war manifested itself when three Type 14 Frigates, a new class of warship for anti-submarine purposes, the HMS *Dundas*, *Exmouth* and *Grafton*, were launched.

By 1954 the Pilot Vessel *Matthew Flinders* was launched for the Queensland Government of Australia while around the same time three 'U'- and 'V'-class wartime destroyers were modified as the newly designated Type 15 Frigates. This involved a complete reconstruction and full conversion. The ships were stripped down to main deck level, extending a new superstructure afterwards, with additional decks, and mounting an entirely new armament.

That year saw the acquisition of the first of two significant subsidiaries, the William Weatherhead yard at Cockenzie on the Firth of Forth. Two years later, the Henry Bannister ropeworks at Cowes was also taken over.

Moving on to 1958, that year saw two more Type 14 Frigates under construction for the Indian Navy, the *Khukri* and *Kuthar*. By the end of the 1950s the yard's order books were full and all slipways occupied. They were indeed halcyon days for the company! But all too briefly.

White's largest cargo vessel, the *Susan Constant*, was launched on 10 December 1957 and HMS *Londonderry*, a new Type 12 Frigate, slid down the ways six months later in May 1958.

This contract led to an order for a frigate of the same type from the Royal New Zealand Navy, HMNZS *Taranaki*, which was launched during August 1959.

Further substantial orders were obtained in 1958 from first-time customers. The first of these was for four large lighthouse tenders for the Corporation of Trinity House for delivery between 1960 and 1964. The lead ship *Mermaid* was followed by the *Siren*, *Stella* and *Winston Churchill*, all of which went on to give sterling service. Concurrent with this contract, White's received an order from the British Transport Commission for two cross-Channel passenger steamers for its Channel Islands service. This was the first such order from the BTC for up to that time its ferries had been built, almost without exception, by William Denny of Dumbarton, its preferred builder. The result was two aesthetically pleasing, luxuriously appointed ships, the *Caesarea* and *Sarnia*, which entered service in 1961 and 1962 respectively.

In March 1961, notwithstanding the fact that the revolutionary combined gas and steam-driven General Purpose Frigate HMS *Eskimo* was launched that month, 140 men were laid off, a hint of trouble ahead. The situation was stabilised but not totally relieved by orders to refit the Antarctic Survey vessel HMS *Protector* and the destroyer HMS *Charity* for the Pakistan Navy.

During 1962 the firm received an order for the 'Leander'-class Frigate HMS *Arethusa*, the last ever warship order the yard would receive from the Admiralty. The company was entering a period of steep decline despite a reprieve in 1964 in the form of the complete overhaul and update of two destroyers for the Egyptian Navy, the *El Fateh* and *El Qaher*. The latter was returning to Cowes for the second time having been converted from the destroyer HMS *Myngs* six years previously. Nevertheless, later that same year the Boatbuilding Department was permanently closed down.

In July 1965 HMS *Arethusa* was completed and delivered, thus bringing down the curtain on a 269-year association with the Admiralty, which in 1964 had become the Ministry of Defence (Navy). Four months later shipbuilding ceased altogether at East Cowes and the Falcon shipyard was closed and sold. The following year the Foundry and the galvanising shop were closed but White's continued building steam turbines for Royal Navy ships until 1969, when the trend for warship propulsion systems switched to gas turbines.

One may well speculate on the true reasons for White's closure. Granted there may have been a world slump in shipbuilding at the time; granted there was always extra cost involved in importing all the required raw materials and different forms of metal from the mainland; granted White's could not compete with the speed and cost of construction of foreign yards to win commercial orders; and granted also that the yard had not reinvested in covered slipways as was being done in other yards throughout the UK, although to some extent space restrictions made it difficult to do this. Nevertheless, the expertise, skills, workforce and the will to succeed were all there and the company's reputation for the quality of its destroyers and frigates was never in question. It was also the very time when the offshore oil industry was about to rapidly expand, with a burgeoning demand for vessels like the latterly completed *South Shore*.

White's demise occurred around the time of the closure of the Fairfields shipyard on the Clyde which became a political issue. No doubt White's predicament was overshadowed by what, in shipbuilding terms, was a bigger affair.

Whatever the reason for the cessation of ship construction and repair at Cowes, it was over half a century ago that the riveting and caulking machines fell silent, the crackling of arc welders and the clatter of chipping hammers following shortly after. The slipways, the foundry, the plating and welding shops and the engine works are all now long gone and all that remains of a once productive heavy industry is the hammerhead crane that stands as a silent sentinel to the Island's proud shipbuilding heritage.

The return to peacetime heralded an immediate decline in naval orders for the main shipyard as had happened back in the 1920s and a number of un-started Admiralty orders were cancelled. Once again, White's pursued commercial contracts to augment whatever naval business it was still able to win and the company secured the order for two 3,950 gross ton refrigerated cargo ships for Société Générale de Transports Maritimes (SGTM), Marseilles, the sisters *Sidi Mabrouk* (yard No.1943) and *Sidi Okba* (yard No.1944). The first picture shows the *Sidi Mabrouk* prior to launch … (Keith MacDonald)

... while the second view, showing the *Sidi Okba* at the fitting-out quay on 29 March 1948, provides an impression of their appearance at delivery, in April and October 1948 respectively. (Authors' collection)

The Argentine cargo vessel *Artico* (yard No.1958) is seen here being launched on 2 December 1948. Prior to delivery she was renamed *Rio Quequen*. She was withdrawn from service in 1978. Her sister the *Antartico* (yard No.1959) was later renamed *Rio Santiago*. (Bernard Taylor)

Here the two sister ships are seen side by side at the fitting-out berth nearing completion in 1949, the *Artico* outboard and *Antartico* inboard. (Bernard Taylor)

Photographed in the Thames in July 1967, the *Rio Santiago*, ex-*Antartico* and her sister were owned by the Argentine Government and operated on its behalf by Flota Mercante del Estado. The *Rio Santiago* was destroyed by fire at Buenos Aires on 13 July 1976. (Kenneth W. Wightman)

▲ One of the company's innovative ideas was the 26ft hand-propelled lifeboat. The photograph clearly shows sixteen men from the boatbuilding shop operating the long hand crank which appears to be geared to the single propeller. This type of propulsion was thought to be better than oars which were disposed of and an improvement on the earlier Fleming Thwartless lifeboat with its patented hand-propelled gear in the form of levers. The lifeboat appears to be built of fibreglass, a mode of construction that was increasingly adopted by White's for boats and other marine products. (Ron Trowell; courtesy of Isle of Wight Heritage Service)

◄ The motor barge *XXXX* (yard No.1962), built for the Mew, Langton & Co. brewers in 1948, is seen moored alongside the quay at Newport, Isle of Wight. In those days, before the advent of large vehicle ferries on the cross-Solent routes, barge traffic was the primary means of conveying commercial produce and heavy machinery between the Isle of Wight and the mainland. White's had set up its own transport subsidiary in 1922 as the Island Transport Co., initially to operate between the Cowes shipyard and the Repair Department in Southampton. Progressively, commercial business was also handled. (Ray Sprake)

A view of one of the boat-building shops in the late 1940s, with two 47ft Watson-type lifeboats under construction for the Royal National Lifeboat Institution, the *Winston Churchill* (yard No.5399) on the left. The other boat could be the *Tynesider* (yard No.5398). The *Winston Churchill* was the *Civil Service No.8* lifeboat raised from Civil Service funds and given Official No.853, stationed at Blyth from 1948–79. (Isle of Wight Heritage Service)

An unusual project undertaken by White's in the late 1940s was the construction of floating docking pontoons for the flying boat maintenance base at Hythe, part of the former Vickers Supermarine Works, and at the BOAC flying boat terminus at Berth 50 in Southampton's Old Docks, the latter, shown here, inaugurated on 14 April 1948. The pontoons remained in use through to the closure of the terminus on 20 December 1958. (*Southern Echo*)

Seen berthed together at the north end of the Thetis shipyard, West Cowes, are the Island Transport Co.'s motor barges *Calbourne* (yard No.1965) – second of the name – and *Shalfleet* (yard No.2012), built by J. Samuel White in 1952 and 1962 respectively. The third barge is the *Arreton*, which was acquired second hand when the Island Transport Co. was formed. All three passed to the Vectis Transport Co. in 1974. (Mick Lindsay)

The twin-screw refrigerated cargo motorship *Kadoura* (yard No.1966), another significant vessel built by White's, was launched on 5 July 1951. Designed for the carriage of bananas in an insulated space of 190,000 cu. ft, she had accommodation for twelve passengers. She was built for the Compagnie Maritime des Chargeurs Réunis of Paris, the third order for a French merchant vessel since the war. (Stewart Bale; courtesy of Isle of Wight Heritage Service)

The 4,143 gross ton *Kadoura* had an overall length of 359ft 3in. She was driven by twin eight-cylinder Burmeister & Wain diesels with an output of 6,500 bhp. She entered service in January 1952 operating between French ports, West Africa and the Canary Islands. (Topic Press; courtesy of Isle of Wight Heritage Service)

A White's advert from 1953 proudly proclaims that six of its ships had been present at the Coronation Review of the fleet in June that year. The image is of HMS *Dainty* in calm waters without her pennant number D 108 displayed, suggesting that it was taken before she was commissioned on 26 February 1953. The *Dainty* was scrapped in 1972. (Authors' collection)

With an abundance of work in the Cowes boatshops, for sixteen inshore minesweepers besides other craft, the company transferred the construction of HMS *Edlingham* (yard No. 5456) to William Weatherhead & Sons of Cockenzie, a yard taken over in 1954. The *Yaxham* (yard No. 5463) was also entrusted to the Scottish yard. They were both 'Ham'-class inshore minesweepers, of 120 tons standard displacement and 106ft 6in length overall. Given the pennant number M2623, the *Edlingham* is seen here afloat on the Forth, probably at her launch on 21 July 1955. (*The Scotsman*; courtesy of Isle of Wight Heritage Service)

Another 'Ham'-class inshore minesweeper, HMS *Nettleham* (yard No. 5462) is about to be launched into the River Medina on 19 December 1956. The Admiralty contract with White's was for thirteen 'Ham-class' craft. Of broadly similar layout and dimensions, White's also built three similar-sized 'Ley'-class minesweepers. Of the total number, ten minesweepers were of all wooden construction and six had wooden hulls over aluminium framing. (Isle of Wight Heritage Service)

Besides the steady demand for destroyer refits and destroyer to frigate conversions that occupied the yard throughout the 1950s, the first orders for new naval ships were also secured at that time, beginning with the three 'Blackwood'-class ASW frigates, HMS *Dundas*, *Exmouth* and *Grafton* (yard Nos 1969–1971). Shown here is HMS *Dundas* (yard No.1969) which was launched on 25 September 1953 and delivered in March 1956. (Ron Trowell; courtesy of Keith MacDonald)

The Admiralty ordered two new fast patrol boats in 1950, one each from J. Samuel White and Vospers at Portsmouth, the *Bold Pioneer* (yard No.5415) and *Bold Pathfinder*. Nominally sisters, the *Bold Pioneer* had a hard chine planing hull, akin to the wartime-built MTBs, whereas the *Bold Pathfinder* had a rounded bilge hull. As such, they were largely experimental, intended to evaluate hull designs to determine the most effective and efficient configuration for achieving high speed in future craft. Here *Bold Pioneer* is shown at speed. (Keith MacDonald)

The *Volage* was taken in hand in 1952 and converted by her builders from a destroyer to a 'V'-class or Type 15 anti-submarine frigate (yard No.1972). In doing this her displacement increased to 2,100 tons and her overall length to 362ft 9in. In her new role she carried two 4in guns, two 40mm Bofors AA guns and two 'Squid' triple-barrelled anti-submarine depth charge mortars. Here she is seen on completion of her conversion with increased superstructure and the pennant number F41. Two other destroyers converted to frigates by White's were HMS *Undaunted* (yard No.1976) and *Troubridge* (yard No.1993). (Beken of Cowes)

Completed in April 1954 for the Government of Nigeria and subsequently extensively modified at the White's yard was the 544 displacement ton survey ship *Pathfinder* (yard No.1975), here seen on trials in The Solent. She was launched on 23 October 1953 and remained in service with the Nigerian authorities until she was stricken in 1975. (Ron Trowell; courtesy of Isle of Wight Heritage Service)

On 8 March 1954 the *Matthew Flinders* (yard No.1977) was launched for the Queensland Government in Australia. She was similar in style to the Trinity House Pilot vessel *Bembridge*, but longer at 200ft 5in. She operated out of Brisbane, maintaining the buoyage in the approaches to ports on the Queensland coast. (Ron Trowell; courtesy of Isle of Wight Heritage Service)

It is understood that late in her career, the *Matthew Flinders*, seen here on pre-delivery trials in The Solent, was modified for inter-island passenger ferry service in the Pacific. She was lost on 11 July 1989 when she was wrecked on the Navatu Reef, south-east of Moala Island, Fiji. (Beken of Cowes)

The exterior of the Henry Bannister's rope 'manufactory' in Mill Hill Road, Cowes, a local company taken over by J. Samuel White in 1956. (Charles Taylor)

This view of the ropewalk at Bannister's, which ran in a southerly direction for approximately 600ft behind the building frontage, as far as and slightly beyond Bridge Road, provides a vivid indication of the rather basic nature of the rope works. The fibre-spinning trolley travelled on rails laid on the earth floor in a long shed that lacked frills and was covered by a corrugated tin roof. Despite the basic working conditions, the Bannister's rope works produced large quantities of quality rope products in sisal, hemp and manila as well as coir fenders. The company also made ropes from nylon and terylene, as well as other plastic-based artificial fibres that floated. (Charles Taylor)

A valuable contract awarded to White's in 1954 was for the single-screw, 223 gross ton, 102ft overall length steam tug *Kestrel* (yard No.1980) from J.P. Knight Ltd of Rochester, Kent, for whom the company had built three tugs in the 1930s. She was driven by an eight-cylinder British Polar Engine which developed 1,150 bhp. In the 1970s she was sold by Knights to Caledonian Towage at Invergordon and she remained based there until she was scrapped in February 1984 by Luguria Marine, Milton Creek, Kent. (Kenneth W. Wightman)

Based on the Royal Navy's 'Blackwood'-class, the frigates *Khukri* (yard No.1987) and *Kuthar* (yard No.2000), the latter shown here, were built for the Indian Navy. The *Kuthar*, which had been launched on 14 October 1958, was completed in July 1959, a year to the month after her sister ship. (Ron Trowell)

Using the same hull form as the 'Ham'-class inshore minesweepers and launched from the boat shop on 1 May 1957, HMS *Echo* (yard No.5465) was a specialist vessel with the rather long-winded title of Admiralty Geographical and Hydrographical Survey Inshore Craft or, for short, Inshore Survey Craft with the pennant number A70. In 1986 she was acquired by the Marine Society and converted to a training ship renamed the *Earl of Romney*. She still survives at Alexandria, under Egyptian ownership, with her name shortened to *Romney*. (Graham Hayes)

The ASW Type 12 frigate *Londonderry* (yard No.1995) of the 'Rothesay'-class was laid down on 15 November 1956, launched on 20 May 1958 and completed on 18 October 1961. She had a displacement tonnage of 2,100 and an overall length of 370ft. Armament was two 4.5in guns and two triple-barrelled anti-submarine mortars. After twenty-eight years of navy service, she was paid off and sunk as a target on 25 June 1989. (Ron Trowell; courtesy of Keith MacDonald)

A boatyard advertisement, dating from 1958, showing an RNLI lifeboat being built. The ribs have been erected in readiness for the strakes. (Authors' collection)

J. SAMUEL WHITE & CO. LTD.

SHIPBUILDERS A'ND ENGINEERS

Strength and Craftsmanship

HEAD OFFICE:
**COWES
ISLE OF WIGHT**
Telephone: COWES 103

LONDON OFFICE:
**GOLDEN CROSS HOUSE
3, DUNCANNON STREET
LONDON W.C.2**
Telephone: TRAFALGAR 5064

The launch of the large engines-aft cargo ship *Susan Constant* (yard No.1996), which was performed by Mrs Margaret Constant on 10 December 1957. In this view the old Red Funnel tug *Neptune* assists the *Susan Constant* by manoeuvring alongside. In the meantime another tug, the *Tampeon*, sent to assist the launching but out of the picture, has fouled the chains of the Cowes floating bridge. (Richard P. de Kerbrech)

The *Susan Constant* was delivered to Constants Ltd, London, in May 1958. Of 3,464 gross tons and 353ft overall length, she was employed on general tramping duties. Sold on by Constants in 1973, she was broken up in 1989 as the *Chiloe IV* after several previous changes of ownership. (Ron Trowell; courtesy of Keith MacDonald)

The General Purpose (GP) or Type 81 (generally referred to as the 'Tribal'-class) frigate HMS *Eskimo* (yard No.2001) broke new ground for White's. She had a single shaft geared to a steam turbine of 15,000 shp and a gas turbine of 7,500 shp in an arrangement known as COSAG. As such, the *Eskimo* was a unit of one of the first major classes of Royal Navy warships to take gas turbines to sea. The 'Tribal'-class combined the functions previously undertaken by the Type 12 (anti-submarine), Type 41 (anti-aircraft) and Type 61 (aircraft direction) frigates, reducing considerably the cost that would have been incurred by equipping the fleet with those specialised vessels. The *Eskimo* was commissioned on 21 February 1963 with pennant number F119. (Michael Cassar)

A view of the East Cowes slipways on 25 March 1959 shows a busy scene with no fewer than four ships under construction. From the left, they are: THV *Siren*, HMNZS *Taranaki*, THV *Mermaid* and RMS *Caesarea*. (Ron Trowell)

One of the most valuable contracts awarded to White's in the late 1950s was the order for four diesel-electric lighthouse tenders for the Corporation of Trinity House. The lead ship was the *Mermaid* (yard No.2002), followed by the *Siren* (yard No.2003), the latter seen here just prior to her launch on 17 September 1959. Their primary role was the replenishment of lighthouse and lightship stations and associated crew relief. (Ron Trowell; courtesy of Isle of Wight Heritage Service)

HMNZS *Taranaki* was an improved 'Rothesay'-class or Type 12 frigate ordered by the Royal New Zealand Navy, launched on 19 August 1959 and commissioned in March 1961. She was powered by high-pressure steam turbines, had the latest hull form with twin rudders and her armament consisted of two triple A/S mortars, twin radar controlled 4.5in guns and twelve 21in torpedo tubes. The accommodation was the most modern and comfortable of its day whereby bunks entirely replaced hammocks and the ship had full air conditioning throughout. (Ron Trowell; courtesy of Keith MacDonald)

The third vessel of the 'Mermaid'-class, the *Stella*, was launched on 1 May 1961 and entered service that October. With the exception of the fourth ship, the *Winston Churchill*, which had modifications incorporated in her structure, these tenders measured 1,425 tons gross and measured 221ft overall length. Their long foredeck, dominated by the large foremast and lifting derrick, was distinctive, being vital to their secondary function of buoy overhaul and maintenance. The *Stella* is seen here in The Solent during pre-delivery trials. (Ron Trowell; courtesy of Keith MacDonald)

Another major order received by White's came from the British Transport Commission for two twin-screw turbine ferries for the Weymouth to Channel Islands service, the sister ships *Caesarea* and *Sarnia*. The result was possibly the largest and best-appointed railway ferries ever to be built for this route. Here, the *Caesarea* (yard No.2008) is seen fitting out alongside the West Cowes quay in late 1960. A point of interest is the ships' hull colour scheme which was modified prior to entry into service. The original design, shown here, had the black paint on the hull level with the main deck along its entire length. In contrast, the scheme that was finally adopted on delivery had the black hull paint carried up an additional deck along the length of the central superstructure. (Ron Trowell; courtesy of Keith MacDonald)

Of the two cross-Channel steamers, the first to enter service with British Railways Southern Region was the *Caesarea*, in November 1960. She had been launched on 29 January of that year. Measuring 4,174 gross tons on a length of 322ft, she and the *Sarnia* could be considered improvements on the *Normannia* which had been built nine years earlier by William Denny at Dumbarton for the Southampton to Le Havre service. The *Caesarea* is pictured in Sealink colours. (John Edgington)

▲▶ The *Sarnia* (yard No.2009), shown here in her original British Railways livery, and her sister *Caesarea* had an aesthetically pleasing design. They were fitted with a bow rudder and anti-roll stabilisers to counteract the bad weather in the Channel and for manoeuvring in the strong tides and currents off the Channel Islands. In 1981 the *Sarnia* became the Saudi pilgrim ship *Saudi Golden Star* sailing between Jeddah, Aqaba and Port Said. The ex-*Sarnia* was broken up in Pakistan from early 1988. (Ron Trowell; courtesy of Isle of Wight Heritage Service)

▲ One of the more unusual warships that the company was contracted to refit was HMS *Protector* (yard No.2011), work that was undertaken during 1961. She had originally been completed in 1936 as a net layer but in 1955 she was re-designated as an Antarctic Patrol Ship with Pennant number A146. Unlike her successor HMS *Endurance*, which was painted red and white, the *Protector* patrolled the Southern Ocean in standard warship grey. (Ron Trowell; courtesy of Isle of Wight Heritage Service)

▼ Last of the 'Mermaid'-class, the *Winston Churchill* was slightly different from the earlier three, such that her tonnage was greater at 1,450 gross tons. All four of these White's-built lighthouse tenders were modified later in their careers to permit them to carry helicopters and, by so doing, extend their working lives. This involved bringing the mainmast forward to just abaft the bridge and the fitting of a helicopter landing pad aft, one deck above the main deck. The photograph shows the *Winston Churchill* on trials. (Ron Trowell; courtesy of Keith MacDonald)

This photograph of RNLB *T.G.B.* (yard No. 5520), Official No. 962, shows her for sale in 1985 at the end of her service career. The *T.G.B.* had been delivered to her Longhope Station, in the Orkneys, on 14 April 1962 where she remained until 1969. By the time of her completion, the Watson type had been slightly modified, increasing in length to 47ft. In March 1969, *T.G.B.* was launched to the rescue of a Liberian cargo ship that was in difficulties in mountainous seas. Tragically, the lifeboat capsized in the extreme conditions and all eight members of her crew lost their lives. From 1970–79, following recovery and repair, the RNLB *T.G.B.* was stationed at Arranmore. She is now on permanent display at the Scottish Maritime Museum at Irvine. (Ray Noble; courtesy of David J. Wilkinson)

A break from tradition for White's came in the early 1960s when Hovercraft Development Ltd contracted the company to build its first hovercraft, the *HD-1*, which was constructed of wood in White's boat shop. Driven by twin six-cylinder Rolls-Royce Continental engines and measuring 50ft in length, *HD-1*'s maiden 'flight' took place at Hythe on 23 October 1963. At the time it entered service it was the first non-amphibious, sidewall hovercraft with air cushions at the bow and stern. This photo shows the *HD-1* as it was originally built. At time of writing the *HD-1* is one of the preserved exhibits in the Hovercraft Museum at Lee-on-the-Solent. (Ron Trowell; courtesy of Steve Smith)

The 'Leander'-class Improved Type 12 frigate *Arethusa* (yard No.2015) was both the last naval ship to be built by White's and the very last ship to be delivered by the yard. Categorised as a General Purpose frigate, her class was equipped, like the earlier *Eskimo*, to perform anti-submarine, anti-aircraft and aircraft direction duties. Laid down on 17 September 1962 and launched on 5 November 1963, her displacement tonnage was 2,350 and her main dimensions were 373ft length overall by 41ft beam. Her main propulsion system was twin-shaft steam turbines giving a speed of 28 knots. (Ron Trowell; courtesy of Isle of Wight Heritage Service)

A contract received by White's to refit two Egyptian destroyers resulted in the *El Fateh* (yard No.2021), ex-HMS *Zenith*, and *El Qaher* (yard No.2022), ex-HMS *Myngs*, being given a full overhaul from May 1963 to July 1964. It was rumoured at the time that so poor was the condition of both destroyers that the firm offered to build them a new 'Leander'-class frigate for the same price as the refit of the two destroyers would cost. (Ron Trowell; courtesy of Isle of Wight Heritage Service)

One of the last private motor yachts to be constructed in the shipyard, ordered by F.M. Brown of Cowes, the *Caramba* (yard No.2013) remains in active operation fifty years after she first entered service, and was for some time berthed at Port Pendennis Marina, Falmouth. Constructed of steel in the 'submarine' shed at East Cowes, the 56 gross ton twin-engined vessel was delivered in May 1962. Her engines are 127 hp Gardner diesels. Her main particulars are hull length of 63ft and beam of 16ft. (Ron Trowell; courtesy of Isle of Wight Heritage Service)

The RNLB *William Henry & Mary King* (yard No.5544) was a 37ft Oakley type lifeboat – the fourth of the type – the 134th and last ever lifeboat to be built for the RNLI by White's with the Official No.980. She was delivered to her station at Cromer, Norfolk, in October 1964. Later, she was transferred to Bridlington in 1967, where she stayed until 1989. From 1989 to 1990 she was relief boat at North Sunderland. (David J. Wilkinson)

The penultimate vessel on the yard list was the 950 gross ton motor coaster *Crescence* (yard No.2025). She had been ordered by the London & Rochester Trading Co. Ltd and was launched on 23 October 1964. With a length of 221ft she was the largest coaster to enter the owner's service to that date. Here she is seen sailing from Southampton, with Calshot Spit in the background. (David Reed)

Although not the last ship to be delivered by White's, the *South Shore* (yard No.2026) was the last vessel on the Main Yard List and as such represented the final contract awarded to the shipyard. Ordered by Offshore Marine Ltd, Rochester, the *South Shore* was an offshore supply ship, among the first to be commissioned for the growing offshore oil industry. She was launched on 4 May 1965. (Ron Trowell; courtesy of Isle of Wight Heritage Service)

Seen here on trials, the 760 gross ton *South Shore* entered service in May 1965. The J. Samuel White Company may well have survived longer as a shipbuilder had it been able to secure more orders for craft of this type. (Ron Trowell; courtesy of Isle of Wight Heritage Service)

PART SIX:

1966-82

The final part of this illustrated history of J. Samuel White & Co., Shipbuilders, looks at the firm's fortunes after the closure of the shipyard and its enduring heritage.

The announcement in late November 1965 that the yard was to close, preceded the previous year by the termination of all boat-building activity, came as a devastating blow to the company and was one it had sought desperately to avoid. For the oldest shipyard on the Admiralty List the curtain had come down after 300 unbroken years of naval construction by White's and its predecessors.

A worldwide slump in new orders, accompanied by acutely restricted investment funds and the inability in the limited available space to modernise with prefabrication facilities had perhaps contributed to make the closure inevitable. The discharge of the remaining Shipbuilding Department management that April had made it a certainty. The work to complete the yard's last ship, HMS *Arethusa* – the 252nd vessel built for the Admiralty since 1748 – had to be supervised by managers from the Engineering Department.

But it was not the end for J. Samuel White's as efforts were made to reorganise around the engineering side of the business. Work continued with the manufacture of a broad range of marine products as the company maintained its innovative philosophy. Turbine and compressor construction continued unabated along with boilers, oil strainers, condensers, steam and diesel engines and, primarily from the Somerton works, refrigeration units.

In 1964, White's had commenced the development and manufacture of jet propulsion marine thrusters, based on Major Gill's invention in 1921. The successful installation of the first deep-sea units in 1966 heralded the establishment of a volume production line of White-Gill marine thrusters, as they were marketed. Other innovations that would form the essence of the company's future manufactured output were glass-reinforced plastic (GRP) products, including indicator buoys, and a motorised pilot hoist which had been conceived by a local industrial designer.

The company proposed to retain, as semi-autonomous subsidiaries, the J. Arthur Dixon greetings card firm with premises at Newport, Isle of Wight, and Inverness, Scotland, and the small marine craft builders J. Samuel White (Scotland) Ltd, the former William Weatherhead concern on the Firth of Forth. Another White's subsidiary, Henry Bannister & Co. rope makers, was closed, however, and partial demolition of the ropewalk began in July 1966. The remaining part of the site in Mill Hill road was sold off in 1968. The former Falcon shipyard in East Cowes became the property of British Hovercraft Corporation, part of the Westland Group, while the Medina shipyard and engineering works in West Cowes entered a period of transition from which it finally emerged as a mixed-unit industrial estate.

Part of White's survival plan involved acting as a licensee to the Elliot Turbomachinery Company Inc., part of the giant Carrier Corporation, producing turbo-compressors to its designs. The arrangement continued until the end of 1971 when White's was taken over by the Carrier Corporation, starting the new year as a wholly owned subsidiary of the American concern. As such it continued in operation for another ten years, although the J. Samuel White name itself passed into history on 20 April 1977 when the company was renamed Elliot Turbomachinery Ltd. But to all employees, current and past, the firm was still referred to as 'Sammy Whites'.

Progressively, manufacturing operations were moved from the old shipyard site to the Somerton works which were better suited to the type of work the company was now engaged in. A continuing decline in fortunes necessitated the disposal of the Island Transport Company, whose vessels and goodwill were sold to rivals Vectis Transport.

Four years after the company was renamed, its new owners decided to give up the struggle to keep things going in worsening trading conditions. From the end of 1981 all manufacturing activities on the Isle of Wight ceased. The remaining locally owned sites were disposed of, apart from the Forest Road works of J. Arthur Dixon which was sold to new owners, and the remnants of the much-reduced workforce were paid off.

But that was not the conclusion to the White's story, for some of its speciality product lines were either retained by Elliot's, operating from other sites, or were snapped up by other manufacturing concerns. PE Composites Ltd (formerly the Patrick Engineering Co.) acquired much of the GRP business, including the fabrication of marker buoys, and to this day it continues to make this product. Elliot Turbomachinery persisted with the production of White-Gill marine thrusters until, as recently as 2006, it transferred ownership of the business to Tees Components Ltd of Saltburn, Lincolnshire, a company which for twenty-three years had been a prime subcontractor supplying machined parts and assemblies. As a result the White's name lives on, for today Tees Components is still delivering White-Gill marine thrusters, for bow and stern applications, to prestigious customers around the world.

The heritage of J. Samuel White also survives in another form, in the amazingly large number of White's-built ships and boats that remain in existence almost half a century after the closure of the shipyard and boatyards. Some of these vessels are now preserved, while others remain in working order and gainful employment. The oldest, over 100 years old, are still in excellent condition, a testament to the quality of workmanship that J. Samuel White's always sought to achieve.

Those surviving J. Samuel White-built craft that have been identified are, in alphabetical order:

Batboat III (1912); *Blyskawica* (1937); *Braemar* (1931) – as the *Amphora*; *Calbourne* (1952); *Caramba* (1962); *Cavalier* (1944); *Diligence* (1947); *Echo* (1958) – as the *Romney*; *Grey Goose* (1942) – as the *Anserava*; light vessel No.86 (1931); *Massey Shaw* (1935); *Minnehaha* (1936); MTB 426/Polish S-7 (1944) as houseboat *Thanet*; *Noneta* (1936), steam cutter for HMS *Osborne* (1896); steam pinnaces 199 (1911) and 236 (1892) – the latter as the *Janet*; *Winston Churchill* (1964) – as the *Churchill*; and the *Xarifa II* (1927). There are also forty-two surviving lifeboats.

The White Major Pilot Hoist was one of the company's products from the post-shipyard closure period, here promoted in a trade magazine. Developed from the concept of a local Isle of Wight industrial designer, it was a simple idea and a boon for pilots who had to climb the Jacob's ladder in all weathers and sea states at their own risk. (Authors' collection)

This is the first Fabricated 46M Turbo-Compressor completed in the Boiler Shop by J.Samuel White's for Elliot Turbomachinery in December 1975. The cylindrical compressor housing was made from rolled mild steel onto which the 14in flanges were welded. The welder responsible for its construction, Mr Ken Colebrook, may be seen second from left. The finished compressor was bound for the petrochemical industry. (Ken Colebrook)

Designed to drive a pump or generator, this J. Samuel White-built Gas Expander or single rotor Gas Turbine, photographed pre-delivery, dates from the late 1960s or early 1970s. (Ron Trowell; courtesy of Steve Smith)

The preserved, 31ft-long steam cutter *Osborne* (yard No.1005), on exhibit in Portsmouth Historical Dockyard, was originally completed in 1896 as Steam Cutter No.439 for the Royal Yacht *Osborne*. Driven by a White compound steam engine, she went on to serve on two other Royal Yachts, the *Alexandra* and the *Victoria & Albert III*. Decommissioned in 1936, she was saved from deterioration when acquired in 1959, at which time restoration commenced. Later, in 1972, she was purchased by A.L. (Tony) Spencer who, by 1999, had fully restored her to working order. In 2007 she was placed as a static exhibit in Boathouse No.7. (Richard P. de Kerbrech)

The lifeboat *Lady Forrest* (yard No.1154) remained in active service until 1967, a sixty-four-year working life, since which time she has been preserved following restoration to her original appearance. She is now an exhibit at the Fremantle Maritime Museum at Victoria Quay, Fremantle. The photograph shows the *Lady Forrest* in the year before her retirement, substantially modified from her as-built form (see page 49) in order to meet the unfolding requirements of her extended career. (Alan Pearce, Fremantle Port Authority)

The yard produced large numbers of steam-powered naval pinnaces from the late 1800s through to the beginning of the First World War. They were among the first vessels built by the yard to have White coil-type boilers installed. This is the preserved armed naval pinnace 199 (yard No.1326), at one time named *Treleague*. Measuring 50ft in length by 10ft beam and now fully restored as part of the collection of The Society of Friends of the Royal Naval Museum at Portsmouth, she is the last surviving steam picket boat. (Colin Work – www.pixstel.com)

The most famous ship to be built by J. Samuel White & Co. was undoubtedly the ORP *Blyskawica*, now proudly preserved in Gdynia since she was decommissioned, after a long career, on 1 May 1976. As such she is the oldest preserved destroyer in the world. At regular intervals she has been repainted in the various camouflage colour schemes that were applied to her during her Second World War operational service. This photograph shows her in the Admiralty Disruptive scheme designed for 'A'-class ships, a pattern comprising white, pale blue, grey and green shades. Her superb condition is a further testament of the quality of her construction as well as the attentive care from her custodians. As the company's slogan once declared: 'White's-built, well-built!' (Marek Twardowski)

Another long-term survivor of the White's-built vessels, the retired veteran fire float *Massey Shaw* has been preserved under the stewardship and care of the Massey Shaw Preservation Society. For some years she could be seen moored at Millwall on the River Thames but, latterly, she underwent an extensive refit in Gloucester Docks prior to return to London. (London Fire Brigade)

Late alterations can be seen at Henri Lloyd's shop at 95/96 High Street Cowes, and listen to local radio stations.

3rd to 6th May 2002

In Cowes and East Cowes

The British-Polish Cowes Commemoration

celebrating

The 60th Anniversary of the Polish destroyer ORP Blyskawica's

defence
of
Cowes

(ORP is the Polish equivalent of our HMS and Blyskawica means Lightning)

"The night Poland saved Cowes 4-5th May 1942"

"Noc gdy Polacy uratowali Cowes 4-5 maja 1942"

Each year, the events of 5 May 1942 are commemorated in a joint Polish/British ceremony on the Parade at Cowes, Isle of Wight. On significant anniversaries the celebrations are on a grander scale, as on the sixtieth anniversary in 2002 shown in this programme of events, and on the sixty-fifth anniversary in 2007. The year of publication of this book witnessed the occasion of the seventieth anniversary of the *Blyskawica*'s gallant fight to save the town where she was created. (Authors' collection)

The only surviving British destroyer from the Second World War period is the White's built *Cavalier* (yard No.1928) now preserved and dry-docked at Chatham in the former Naval Dockyard. Acquired by the Cavalier Trust five years after she was decommissioned, to become a museum ship, the efforts to preserve her have taken a lot of time and effort. She finally returned to Chatham in 1998 fully restored for permanent retention as part of the Chatham Historic Dockyard exhibits. One of her propellers remains on display on the sea front at East Cowes. (Graham Nicholls)

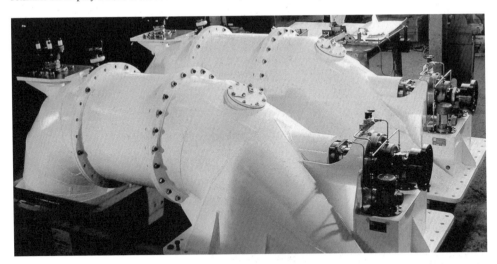

The White-Gill marine thruster (now known as the Elliott White Gill thrust and propulsion unit), was first produced by White's in the early 1960s. Mounted flush with the hull, below a vessel's draft line it is a low head, high volume axial pump capable of delivering thrusts of up to 38,000 pounds (17,000 kg) in every direction – forward, reverse, broadside, and any direction in between. Thrust is produced by drawing water through the intake, and discharging it on an almost horizontal plane through a deflector that rotates a full 360 degrees. Today, these thrusters are still manufactured to the same J. Samuel White specifications by Tees Components Ltd of Saltburn, Cleveland, which acquired the business from Elliott Turbomachinery Ltd in January 2006. (Tees Components Ltd)

Another former White's marine product taken over for continued fabrication after the company's demise is this composite indicator buoy designed for use with submersible craft. With a rigid PVC foam buoyancy core and Glass Reinforced Plastic (GRP) skin, when released it ascends under natural buoyancy to deploy a radio antenna and transmit a distress message on reaching the surface. Today, almost fifty years later, the buoys are still being made by PE Composites on the Daish Way Industrial Estate at Newport, Isle of Wight, which, in 1982, acquired the Glass Reinforced Plastic (GRP) designs and expertise of J. Samuel White & Co. (Ron Trowell; courtesy of PE Composites)

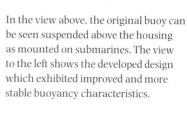

In the view above, the original buoy can be seen suspended above the housing as mounted on submarines. The view to the left shows the developed design which exhibited improved and more stable buoyancy characteristics.

Purchased second-hand and constructed by Babcock & Wilcox of Renfrew, the 80-ton lift cantilevered hammerhead crane was erected in the West Cowes shipyard in 1911 or 1912. It is now a listed structure and remains a distinctive landmark for the town of Cowes. Intense efforts are being made to preserve the crane in situ as a lasting monument to the J. Samuel White shipyard which was once a major source of local employment. (David L. Williams)

SELECT BIBLIOGRAPHY

Adams, R.B., *Red Funnel and Before* (Kingfisher Railway Productions, 1986)

Barnaby, K.C., *100 Years of Specialized Shipbuilding & Engineering* (Hutchinson, 1964)

Blackman, Raymond V.B., *The World's Warships* (Macdonald & Co., 1960)

Brouwer, Norman J., *International Register of Historic Ships* (Anthony Nelson, 1993)

Couling, David, *Solent Yachting Scene 1890-1938* (Stanford Maritime, 1984)

         Steam Yachts (Batsford, 1980)

Jung, Ingvar, *The Marine Turbine – Part 1* (National Maritime Museum, 1981)

Lenton, H.T., *British Warships* (Ian Allan Ltd, 1962)

         Warships from 1860 to the Present Day (Hamlyn, 1970)

Lenton, H.T. and College, J.J., *Warships of World War II* (Ian Allan Ltd, 1973)

Langensiepen, Bernd and Guleryuz, Ahmet, *The Ottoman Steam Navy 1828–1923* (Conway Maritime Press, 1995)

Parker, George H., *Astern Business – 75 Years of UK Shipbuilding* (World Ship Society, 1996)

Rowland, K.T., *Steam at Sea* (David & Charles, 1970)

Smith, E.C., *A Short History of Naval & Marine Engineering* (Babcock & Wilcox, 1937)

Talbot-Booth, E.C., *All the World's Fighting Fleets* (Sampson Low, Marston, *c*.1943)

Williams, David L., *White's of Cowes* (Silver Link Publishing, 1993)

         Wings over the Island (Coach House Publications, 1999)

Miscellaneous Papers

J. Samuel White Yard Lists as compiled by:

Isle of Wight County Archive.

Captain John Landels (World Ship Society).

Raymond F. Sprake.

Unpublished notes on J. Samuel White & Co. by Frank C. Bowen.

If you enjoyed this book, you may also be interested in...

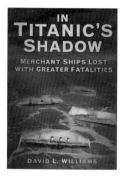

In Titanic's Shadow

DAVID L. WILLIAMS

Each of the merchant ships here had a greater number of casualties than *Titanic's* 1,500, accounting for a total of 96,000 lives lost. Included are the *Lancastria*, Britain's worst maritime disaster with 3,000 lost; the *Ryusei Maru*, a Japanese 'Hellship' loaded with 6,000 Allied POWs, torpedoed by a US submarine; and the *Wilhelm Gustloff*, a German liner packed with 7,800 civilians, sunk by a Russian submarine, a tragedy which was the worst maritime disaster of all time.

978-0-7524-7122-8

Belfast Built Ships

JOHN LYNCH

Belfast has a long and proud shipbuilding heritage, having been home to three main shipbuilders: Harland & Wolff, Workman Clark and McIllwain & Co., all of whom had fascinating and often turbulent histories. Despite this, little is known about the vessels they produced, beyond the world-famous story of *Titanic*. This exhaustively researched book endeavours to change this, revealing the fascinating stories of the many ships to be built and launched from Belfast over the years.

978-0-7524-6539-5

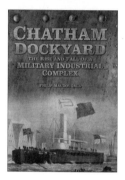

Chatham Dockyard

PHILIP MACDOUGALL

Founded in 1570, Chatham Dockyard quickly became one of the most important British naval yards, building and maintaining warships on the River Medway for the next 400 years. In this detailed history from experienced maritime author Philip MacDougall, particular attention is given to the final 200 years of the yard's lifetime, the artisans and labourers who worked there and the changing methods used in the construction of some of the finest warships to enter naval service.

978-0-7524-6212-7

Merchant Shipping: 50 Years in Photographs

DAVID HUCKNALL

Merchant shipping was once dominated by vessels of well-established companies following regular routes at predictable intervals. The sixties, however, marked the start of the container 'revolution' and, with it, the redundancy of fleets of relatively modern, fast, cargo liners. This book is a collection of David Hucknall's superb black-and-white photographs of ships from across the globe, along with well-researched captions, all collected over a lifetime as a shipping enthusiast.

978-0-7524-5623-2

Visit our website and discover thousands of other History Press books.

www.thehistorypress.co.uk